Religious Drama 2

RELIGIOUS DRAMA 2

Mystery and Morality Plays

Selected and Introduced

by E. MARTIN BROWNE

LIVING AGE BOOKS

published by MERIDIAN BOOKS, INC.　*New York*

E. MARTIN BROWNE

E. Martin Browne, the editor of RELIGIOUS DRAMA 2, *has long been associated with the revival of the religious drama in the twentieth century. He had already staged a number of such productions when he was appointed the first Director of Religious Drama in England, by the Bishop of Chichester in 1930. He has directed and produced the first showings of all the plays of T. S. Eliot; also several plays of Charles Williams and Christopher Fry. Mr. Browne has edited numerous plays from the medieval English dramatic cycles, and it was under his direction that the York Cycle was revived in 1951, and shown again in 1954 and 1957 at the York Festival. He was created C.B.E. in 1952.*

Acknowledgments

The plays from the York Cycle are reprinted from *The York Cycle of Mystery Plays* edited by Dr. J. S. Purvis, by permission of The Macmillan Company, New York. *The Sacrifice of Isaac* and *The Parliament of Heaven: The Annunciation and Conception,* edited by E. Martin Browne, are reprinted by permission of SPCK, London. The plays from the Cornish Cycle are reprinted from *The Legend of the Rood,* edited by F. E. Halliday, by permission of Gerald Duckworth & Company, Ltd., London. *Everyman* is reprinted from *Three Medieval Plays,* edited by John Allen, by permission of William Heinemann Ltd., London.

A Living Age Books Original
Published May 1958 by Meridian Books, Inc.
First Printing April 1958
Second Printing August 1959
Third Printing July 1960

CONTENTS

Introduction by E. MARTIN BROWNE

I want to invite my readers to return with me on a late May day to the great city of York as it was five hundred and fifty years ago. It will mean arising early—in the imagination only—and taking a walk on the city wall above what is now a large railroad junction. This is the highest point of the wall, since the land rises to a slight eminence on the west side of the river, and we can see from our point of vantage over the whole city. In the center of it rises the great Minster which still forms a landmark of the city and the whole surrounding countryside.

Around the Minster are a huddle of streets, very narrow, very fetid, with houses and numerous churches whose spires and towers we can see rising above them. From these churches we can also hear the sound of innumerable bells, for it is the great feast of Corpus Christi, recently instituted to honor Jesus in the sacrament of the Last Supper, and everyone in the city must go to Mass. There is another and more special reason why they should do so, for on this day the Mystery Plays are given and many of the citizens of York are taking part in one of the forty-eight which form the cycle of plays given from dawn until dusk.

Outside the wall of the city we see a scene of great animation. Where the forecourt of the railroad station now stands there is a rough grassy sward. It is called "Pageant Green." On it hundreds of men are running hither and thither with great verve and purpose; and into it a series of great carts, all of them with different superstructure, some one storey high, some two, all elaborately decorated, are being pulled from sheds that surround its edge. These are the "pageants" on which the plays will be performed, for each play is a one-act representing a single scene in the history of the world. Each play has its own

7

stage, its own moving stage on wheels, and they follow one another round the city to twelve stations or stopping places at which the plays are given in order. The first performance is due to begin at four-thirty A.M., and the last will be lighted by torches as dusk falls in the evening.

Most of the men to be seen are wearing the ordinary clothes of their time, but among them are a large number who have special costume for their plays. We can concentrate our attention on one wagon which seems to be further advanced in its preparations than the rest. This is a two-storey wagon, evidently representing Heaven above and Hell beneath. Ready to move with it are a figure in a majestic costume topped with a triple crown, angels and devils. As it seems to be moving off, we can walk round the wall to the nearest "bar" or gate into the city, and see this pageant as it enters.

The bar is called Micklegate Bar and it still stands at the point where the road from York leaves the city to go to Leeds. The pageant lumbers round the corner up the hill, followed by its actors in procession. As it passes through the gate it has a tight squeeze to negotiate the top of the arch and then, moving along the street, comes to rest in front of Holy Trinity Priory, Micklegate. A considerable crowd is already gathered and people are hanging out of all the windows. The actor who plays God the Father ascends the pageant and in two lines of majestic Latin sets the tone of the performance which is to last throughout the day.

> *Ego sum Alpha et O, Vita, Via,*
> *Veritas, Primus et Novissimus.*

Leaving the performers for a moment, it is well to inquire how all this came about. What are the origins of this popular and elaborate dramatic festival? For hundreds of years before this time the Church had been using dramatic forms which had arisen from the liturgy of the Church's year. At the festival of Easter the visit of the Marys to the sepulchre to discover that it was empty had been dramatized in the service itself, and correspondingly,

① Two marys
② Mage Shepherds

soon after, the visit of the shepherds to the crib. Around these gradually grew an elaborate display of the story of these two great festivals. Many other dramatic forms incorporated within the Church's services developed after them. The people naturally wished to have a share in this manner of showing forth their faith, for we must not believe that the people were so ignorant as they have been made out to be. True, most of them could not read, but they received regular instruction and the plays show that they must have had a very extensive and accurate knowledge of the Bible, derived from the plays themselves, from instruction they had received in Church, and from the stories which were passed on in families from parents to children.

The result of all this was that gradually great popular festivals of plays, such as that of York, grew up in which elements dealing with particular scenes from the Bible were gathered together to form a pattern of human history. It was characteristic of the Middle Ages to arrange events in patterns. Order was the foundation of life. In a time of insecurity this was natural, but furthermore it was the conception which grew from the international Christian society of the Church. And so when they dramatized the history of the world, it was as the working out of God's plan. The York cycle is the only complete example that remains, but such cycles grew up in a great many places, showing forth in a single day the whole of the history of the world from a Christian point of view.

The people of the Middle Ages were organized through their crafts, and the plays were performed by the craft guilds. The craft guilds were societies of master craftsmen with apprentices, some of them very powerful and very rich, many of them having their own chapels or even their own churches in the city, supporting their own guild halls (some of which still survive), and maintaining their own pageant or their play in the cycle. The corporation of the city controlled the allocation of the plays and tried to give each guild the play most suitable to it. They gave to the shipwrights, for instance, the play of Noah's flood; to the goldsmiths, the play of the three kings who required crowns and gifts; to the makers and users of nails, the nailing of Christ to the cross. In this manner the skill of each craft was used for the purpose of its play, and there is no doubt that they vied with each other in producing the most magnificent and the most telling results. The corporation laid down the order of playing, the stations at which the performances should be given and the rules under which they should operate. We still have the proclamation which was delivered before the performance each year, which runs in part like this:

> "We command on the King's behalf and the Mayor and the Sheriff's of this city, that no man go armed in this city with swords, nor with carlillaxes, nor none other defences in disturbance of the King's peace and the play."

And then it speaks to those who put on the plays:

> ". . . that all manner of craftsmen bring forth their pageants in order and course by good players well arrayed and openly speaking upon pain of losing a hundred shillings to be paid to the Chamber without any pardon and that every player that shall play be ready in his pageant at convenient time, that is to say at the mid hour between the fourth and fifth of the clock in the morning and then all other pageants fast following one after the other as their course is without tarrying."

Returning to the play in progress in front of Holy Trinity, Micklegate, God the Father has just delivered his opening two lines in Latin. After these lines, the actor exchanged Latin for the English vernacular. The plays which used to be given in Church were first of all entirely in Latin; only later was some of the "vulgar" tongue introduced along with it. The Mystery Plays, however, were popular drama and were from the first written in the "vulgar" tongue. They employed a few lines of Latin to communicate a sense of the majesty of the subject and of its connection with the liturgy of the Church, but the drama was portrayed in the language of the people who were to see it.

We first behold God the Father, alone in the universe: He has as yet created no being. During this first play He creates the nine orders of angels to surround and worship Him. One of them He singles out as bearer of light, Lucifer; but Lucifer is stricken by pride, wishes to usurp God's place and has to be cast out of Heaven with his followers. The casting out of Lucifer was actually dramatized in the pageant, for God the Father, on the Heavenly level above, casts down Lucifer and his evil angels through a trap door into Hell, depicted on the lower level of the pageant. Immediately quarrels break out between them as the evil principle begins its work, and the central conflict of the whole drama is established —the conflict between good and evil.

The rest of the plays in the cycle may be classified in the light of the pattern which has been initiated. There are five more plays in the York cycle that concern the creation and the fall of Man. The Devil becomes a "worm," as the medieval author calls him; he enters the Garden of Eden to betray Eve and cause her to betray Adam, resulting in their being cast out of Heaven. There follow five plays of Old Testament subjects chosen as foreshadowings of the redemption of Man by the coming of Jesus. The Incarnation itself is treated in no less than nine plays, beginning with a prophetic speech by a doctor expounding how the Old Testament prepares for the Annunciation. After the Annunciation itself, we are shown in very human detail the reactions of Joseph to Mary's pregnancy and the difficulty which he has in understanding it. Then we are taken to Bethlehem to witness the birth of Christ, the visits of the shepherds and the kings, and Herod's massacre of the innocents. Mary and Joseph then flee to Egypt, ending this section of the cycle. There is a play centering upon Christ among the doctors at the age of twelve, and then five plays of His ministry, beginning with the baptism and showing the temptations, the transfiguration, and some of His miracles. The Passion, which is the climax of the cycle, is shown in great detail. Eleven plays are taken to trace the conspiracy of Judas, the agony in the Garden, the betrayal and the various trials, the tortures through which Christ passes as He is fastened to the Cross, His death and burial, and the Harrowing of Hell.

The Resurrection, the original core of the medieval religious drama, is developed in this cycle with a touching and moving humanity, especially as regards the person of Christ Himself. This section of six plays ends with the Ascension. There are then four plays concerning the life of the early Church, one at Pentecost and three focussing upon the Virgin Mary, who became during the later Middle Ages an ever more important person in the minds of Christians. The cycle ends, as it must, with the Last Judgement.

This is the substance and order of the forty-eight plays composing the York cycle. The other cycles in England, and the other religious plays parallel to them on the Continent, all treat essentially the same material. For this is a body of knowledge that men possessed as common property. The Middle Ages was not a time of speculation about the nature of the world, but rather about the nature of things within a world, the character of which had been determined by God, who had given to men all sufficient knowledge of it. Accordingly, the pattern into which these plays fall must inevitably be the same, and the differences between them differences of artistic treatment. All of them share a combination of homeliness and majesty. The sense of the majesty of the pattern is never absent, but equally the sense that as human beings we are part of the pattern, and that by virtue of our full humanity. In view of this fact the individual characters in the plays can be given stronger individual qualities of humor and human understanding. This means that the plays, although they may have had a didactic purpose, are also excellent and lively drama for the most part and remain so today.

The cycles as we have them are, of course, not in their original form. As was inevitable with popular work being performed annually, they underwent constant revision, the earlier simpler work often being overlaid, very much in the manner of Gothic architecture in the English cathedrals and great churches. Some of the developments are for the good, some perhaps weaken and over-decorate the original theme. All the plays are written in verse, some of it simple, some of it extremely elaborate. The later authors have a great love of alliteration, which came to be the principal embellishment of later English medieval poetry. Much of the writing is highly formal, some of it may even appear to be stiff, but this is mixed with an extraordinary directness and naturalness which suddenly brings characters to the most vivid life. People such as the shepherds, the porters, even the torturers who carry out the Crucifixion, live as understandable, knowable, lovable human beings, and there is no line drawn between those characters which can be treated with humanity and those which cannot. There are moments, even in the drawing of Jesus Himself, which have an extremely touching human quality. There are many such moments in the characterization of the Virgin Mary, especially as regards her wifely treatment of Joseph after his failure to understand the coming of her child. There is, too, much comedy in the plays, arising primarily from this individuality of character. Certain figures are allowed to be definitely comic, such as Noah's wife in the plays of Noah's flood. The devils have a comic aspect, but this is not as strong as has often been supposed and must never be allowed to obscure the terror of which they are also vehicles.

As we observed earlier while watching the play in preparation, the costume of most of the people who were busy with it was contemporary. The conception of characters is entirely in contemporary terms. There is no sense of period as we think of it: no sense that because this story actually happened in Palestine a great many years ago the people must therefore appear different. The authors and the actors conceived the stories happening in their own circumstances, as may be seen in innumerable references to local affairs and innumerable ways of doing things which derive from the local life of the Middle Ages. The characters are thought of in terms of their counterparts in the life around the players. Annas and Caiaphas, for instance, are represented as bishops in ecclesiastical copes and mitres, and addressed as bishops by all the other characters. Pilate is thought of as a great lord. At the beginning of the plays in which he appears, he makes boastful speeches about his power and he exercises that power in the manner that one would expect of the owner of feudal estates in the Middle Ages. In fact the whole story is conceived in terms of the English climate, English life in a feudal age, and the English countryside; for we must remember that even in a large city in the Middle Ages, the country was much nearer than it is in a large city today. Many of the citizens would themselves be concerned with farming; there would be agricultural land right up to the walls of the city; agricultural produce would be passing constantly in and out of it; and the country would be a part of the town to a degree which we cannot conceive today.

The "countenance divine" of Jesus does indeed "shine forth among our clouded hills" in the English Mystery Plays, as in all the medieval arts. For it is worth noting too that the Plays had a very powerful influence on the other arts, and that many of the arrangements of scenes which we see in stained glass, in painting, in illumination, in sculpture such as the English alabasters, have quite clearly been derived from the performance of these scenes in the Mystery Plays.

Now we must consider the other cycles which occurred in England in the Middle Ages. The collection presented in this volume is drawn from a number of different sources, but the York cycle, as we have seen, is the only complete collection; forty-eight plays remain, and they cover the whole history of man. All the other cycles doubtless compassed the same scope, but none of them has survived intact. The earliest of them comes from Chester. This cycle consisted of twenty-four plays, many of them longer than the York plays, and is the least revised of all the cycles. Here we can sense, most clearly, the early simple type of play, which was created probably in the thirteenth century and which Chester seems doggedly to have defended from extensive revision in the days of greater elaboration.

Near York is the ancient city of Wakefield, and this also had its own cycle; though the Wakefield cycle shared a number of plays and, it has been thought possible, even derived them from those performed at York. In spite of considerable gaps, it possesses many unique features. Most important of these is the work of one, usually known to scholars as the Wakefield Master, a writer of the fifteenth century who works in an elaborate stanzaic form and possesses a very strong and highly developed sense of comedy. He was evidently a dramatist of great stature.

Coventry is the city which, in popular legend, has become most famous of all for its Mystery Plays—so much so that its name became attached by mistake to a cycle which did not belong to it. Of the Coventry cycle proper, only two plays remain. What is usually known as the Coventry Nativity play—the play of the Shearmen and Tailors' guild—covers the whole story from the Annunciation to the Massacre of the Innocents. The other play is the Weavers'; an elaborate dramatization of the presentation of Christ in the Temple. The cycle to which the name *Ludus Coventriae* was attached by mistake had better be denominated by the name of Hegge, who was long the owner of the manuscript, for it is uncertain from where this cycle derives. Dr. Hardin Craig's suggestion that it is the lost cycle from Lincoln seems on the whole the most plausible. At any rate it is the latest in date of the cycles and the most ecclesiastical in its manner of writing. There is less humanity about it and more theology. Thus it is apt to deal most successfully with those moments in the story which are enshrined in the liturgy. It also introduces the beginnings of what afterwards became the Morality Play, as may be seen in one of the extracts.

Apart from the cycles, quite a number of fragments remain which may either be parts of lost cycles, or plays offered by themselves in smaller places where a cycle would have been too expensive an undertaking. One of these, and an exceptionally beautiful one, from Brome in Suffolk, is included in this collection.

The texts which are used in this volume are, of course, all edited texts, for modern readers would not be able to understand the Middle English. The York plays which form a large part of this collection are taken from the comprehensive edition prepared by Dr. J. S. Purvis and published by S.P.C.K. Dr. Purvis' edition is a complete transcription of the whole forty-eight plays, and those which have been chosen from it are reproduced in their entirety. Dr. Purvis has modernized only so far as was necessary to make the text comprehensible to a modern reader, and he has preserved much of the northern flavor. Many of the expressions found in the plays are still in current use, especially in the countryside north and east of York.

The other English Mystery Plays I have edited from the Middle English texts, in some cases more freely than has Dr. Purvis. I have made certain cuts in them and transcribed certain passages fairly freely where the meaning seemed too obscure. I have, however, been very careful to adhere to the verse pattern and to preserve all that I possibly could of the flavor of the original writing. This I think is an essential qualification for any modern edition. It is all too easy, in doing the necessary work which enables a modern reader to read the plays at all, to take away much of their essential quality almost without realizing that one has done so.

Three of the plays are written in Cornish, which is a separate language akin to Breton and Welsh. These have been translated by Mr. F. H. Halliday. The Morality Play, *Everyman,* has been edited by Mr. John Allen and is reproduced from the edition in Heinemann's Drama Library.

The plan of the book is to follow the structure of a Mystery Play cycle, but to use plays from different cycles in order to show as wide a variety as possible of the writing of this type and period. The first group of plays, following the one which we have tried to watch in imagination as its performance began, concerns the creation and fall of Man. These are taken from the York cycle and manifest the high quality of art which this cycle contains. They show the beginning of the conflict between good and evil in the life of Man and the necessity for redemption through the life, death and resurrection of our Lord Jesus Christ. From the Old Testament we have three plays on subjects chosen because of their anticipatory reference to that redemption. The play of Noah's flood comes from Chester and is one of the most characteristic works of that cycle—rugged, humorous, genuinely spiritual. The stage directions are translated from the original Latin and give a vivid indication of how the play was actually performed. The ark, which was built upon the pageant wagon, was obviously in the form of a medieval ship, with a "top castle" or castellated cabin, and was covered with "slitch" (or as we call it, pitch) to keep out the water.

The play of Abraham and Isaac from Brome is distinguished by a more poignant exposition of human emotions than is found in any other version. It has many correspondences with that in the Chester cycle, from which it may well have been elaborated.

The Cornish play about David forms part of the Legend of The Rood, which traces the origin of the wood of the Holy Cross from shoots planted by Moses that had sprouted from the seeds placed in Adam's mouth at his death.

Passing to the life of Christ, the series begins with a play of the Annunciation from the latest of the cycles, the Hegge cycle. This opens with a prologue which foreshadows the Morality Play, wherein four abstract Virtues contend about the state of Man and finally agree to appeal to God to save Man by His own intervention. In response to this appeal He sends Gabriel to Mary and the conception of Christ is represented on the stage. How the extremely graphic stage direction given at this point was carried out is difficult to determine. This play reminds us of the depictions of the Annunciation by the early Renaissance painters of Florence and Siena.

The play of the birth of Christ from the York cycle is one of the most beautiful in all medieval literature. The adoration of the new-born Jesus is couched in terms of such absolute faith as well as poetic beauty that it cannot fail to convince even a modern skeptical hearer.

The shepherds always provide one of the finest occasions for exploitation in the cycle, for they give the opportunity for rustic characterization and for the bringing in of local qualities. The Wakefield shepherds' play, famous as it is, cannot be said to be altogether typical, for the Wakefield Master has developed the secular side of the story to an extent not found in any of the other plays. The sheepstealing incident is in fact a farce, and one might feel that the religious scene at its conclusion was merely tacked on to it, if one did not realize that the two things are brought together by being played on the same stage. One end of the pageant must have represented the fields, the other end the cottage, which is first seen as Mac's cottage and later as the stable—so the child Jesus is placed in the same cradle which previously held the stolen sheep. Thus there is complete congruity between the shepherds in their secular quarrel with Mac and their deeply touching, because completely genuine, religious expression of adoration as they bring their gifts to the Christ Child. No better illustration could be found of the integration of religion into the whole of life than this play.

The play of the kings and Herod from the real Coventry cycle is famous because Shakespeare referred to it: Hamlet tells the players that they must not "outherod Herod." It is easy to see from this script that an actor playing Herod would be tempted to overact, and Shakespeare in his youth obviously saw this happen at Coventry. The script has great power, and the madness of Herod is more vividly portrayed here than in any of the other Mystery Plays.

For the adult life of Jesus, I have selected three plays: first, the Temptation from the York cycle, which follows closely the Biblical story but dramatizes both Jesus and Satan with great vividness. Next The Woman Taken in Adultery, which is shown in a more developed form, both as regards plot and character, in the Hegge cycle than in any other. And lastly, Palm Sunday, which is the longest play in the York cycle and includes a number of miracles and incidents leading to the entry into Jerusalem. That entry itself is the occasion of one of the finest pieces of late medieval poetry. The burghers, who correspond to the Lord Mayor and Aldermen of York, emerge from the city gates to welcome their distinguished guest in a series of eight exquisitely beautiful speeches.

The Passion is represented by plays which illuminate the medieval world-view. The banners at the Trial bow perforce to the King of Kings: the toughest soldiers cannot prevent them, and at their second attempt Pilate himself and the Chief Priests are compelled to follow their example. Yet this proof of Jesus' divinity does not save Him from the most brutal treatment by the torturers who scourge and nail Him to the cross.

The Middle Ages were deeply concerned, as we have seen, with the supernatural aspect of the conflict between good and evil, and all the medieval cycles contain a play dealing with the Harrowing of Hell. The clause in the Creed which says that after his burial Jesus "descended into Hell" is interpreted as meaning that He rescued the souls of the faithful who had died before His time and were held by the Devil until He came to release them. This provided a mighty dramatic conflict between Christ and Satan, based on the psalm:

> *Lift up your heads, O ye gates, and be ye lift up,*
> *ye everlasting doors;*
> *And the King of Glory shall come in.*
> *Who is the King of Glory?*
> *The Lord of Hosts, he is the King of Glory.*

Christ breaks down the gates of Hell, frees Adam and Eve and the other Patriarchs, and sends them to heaven with Michael, the archangel who binds Satan.

The Resurrection itself is always treated quietly in the Cycles; the Cornish play of the Three Maries approaches it in a similar spirit, though with a warmth of emotion peculiarly its own. The Ascension becomes an opportunity for Jesus to set forth the nature of His work on earth, and to look forward to the Last Judgement, wherein He, as Judge of the world, pronounces a solemn and moving version of the parable of the sheep and the goats from St. Matthew's Gospel. Thus our skeleton Mystery Cycle comes to an end with the pronouncement by God the Father: "Now is fulfilled all my forethought;" and we see the history of mankind completed according to God's purpose.

The elements of the Morality Play were early visible in the Mysteries, as we have seen in the dialogue of the Four Daughters of God in the Hegge play of the Annunciation. The Morality is an allegory, in which figures representing Virtues and Vices, forces of good and evil, contend for man's soul. Dramatically, this type of play has severe limitations, for no character can behave unexpectedly, even the representative of humankind (*Humanum Genus,* Mankind, Everyman) can only change from good to evil and back again, with none of the complexity of actual human motives. But when handled by a master, the form can produce immortal drama, as in the instance given here. *Everyman* has the further advantage that its action is concentrated: instead of trying to trace the fortunes of mankind through a whole lifetime, it begins at the point where man is confronted with Death, and this gives to the whole play an urgency lacking from some of the other Moralities.

This collection will, I hope, give an idea of the quality and scope of the medieval religious drama. I would urge readers to speak the lines aloud in order to savor their full quality, for what appears difficult to grasp from the printed page will come alive in speaking. The verse forms

and diction are a part of the plays' charm; and to modern-
ize further than is done in these versions would be to
destroy their essential nature. To appreciate them it is
necessary, as with the visual art of the period, to carry
oneself back in imagination to another age: but the re-
wards of doing so are the discovery of a Christian society
whose life can illuminate our own.

THE CREATION OF THE HEAVENLY BEINGS: THE FALL OF LUCIFER

York Tanners' Play

GOD:
Ego sum alpha et O, Vita, Via,
Veritas, Primus et Novissimus.
I am gracious and great, God without a beginning;
I am maker unmade, and all might is in me.
I am life and way unto weal winning;
I am foremost and first; as I bid shall it be.
My blessing in joy shall be blending,
And falls from harm to be hiding;
My body in bliss aye abiding,
Unending without any ending.
Since I am maker unmade, and most high in might,
And aye shall be endless, and nought is but I,
Unto my dignity dear shall duly be dight
A place full of plenty, at my pleasure to ply.
And therewith as I will I have wrought
Many divers doings amain,
Which my work shall duly contain,
And all shall be made even of nought.
But only the worthy work of my will
In my spirit shall inspire the might of me;
And in the first fitly my thoughts to fulfil,
At hand in my blessing I bid that here be
A bliss all-protecting about me.
In the which bliss I bid that be here

Nine orders of angels full clear,
In love everlasting to lout me.

> *Then the angels sing: Te Deum Laudamus te
> dominum Confitemur.*

Here underneath me now an isle do I name,
Which Isle shall be earth now; therefore is all
Earth wholly and Hell, and this high place is Heaven.
All that wealth shall wield shall dwell in this hall;
This grant I you, ministers mine,
While steadfast in thought ye remain;
And also all them that are nought
Shall pine in hell-prison in pain.
Of all mights I have made most near after me,
I make thee as master and mirror of my might;
I set thee here by me in bliss for to be,
And name thee now, Lucifer, as bearer of light.
Nought here shall make thee to fear;
In this bliss shall your dwelling remain;
All wealth in your wielding retain,
The while due obedience you bear.

> *Then the angels sing: Sanctus, sanctus, sanctus,
> Domine Deus Sabaoth.*

FIRST ANGEL SERAPHYN:
Ah, merciful maker, full mickle is thy might,
That all this world at a word worthily hast wrought.
Aye loved be that lovely lord for his light,
That thus us mighty has made, who now were right
   nought.
In bliss for to bide in his blessing,
Everlasting in love let us lout him,
Who sets us thus closely about him,
Of mirth nevermore to have missing.

FIRST ANGEL LUCIFER:
All the mirth that is made is marked in me.

The beams of my brilliance are burning so bright,
And so seemly in sight myself I now see.
Like a lord am I lifted to dwell in this light.
More fairer by far I appear;
In me is no point to impair;
I feel me well favoured and fair;
My power is passing my peers.

FIRST ANGEL CHERUBYN:
Lord, with a lasting love we love thee alone,
You mightiful maker that marked us and made us,
And wrought us thus worthily to dwell as thy own
Where never feeling of filth may foul us nor fade us.
All bliss is here biding about us,
The while we are stable of thought
In the worship of him that us wrought;
Of dread need we never more doubt us.

FIRST ANGEL LUCIFER:
Oh what!
I am favoured and fair and figured full fit;
The form of all fairness upon me is fast.
All wealth I am wielding, so wise is my wit;
The beams of my brightness are built with the best.
My showing is shimmering and shining,
So bigly to bliss am I brought;
I need to annoy me right nought;
Here shall never pain bring me pining.

ANGEL SERAPHIM:
With all the wit that we wield we worship thy will,
Thou glorious God that is ground of all grace.
Aye with steadfast sound let us stand still,
Lord, to be fed with the food of thy fair face.
In life that is truly aye-lasting,
Thy dole, Lord, is aye daintily dealing;
And whoso that food may be feeling,
To see thy fair face, is not fasting.

FIRST ANGEL LUCIFER:
Oh sure, what!
I am worthily wrought with worship, I wis;
For in a glorious glee my glittering it gleams.
I am so mightily made my mirth may not miss;
Aye shall I bide in this bliss through brightness of beams.
I need no annoyance to name;
All wealth at my will am I wielding;
Above all yet shall I dwell in fame,
On height in the highest of heaven.
There shall I set myself, full seemly to sight,
To receive my reverence through right of renown.
I shall be like unto him that is highest on height!
Oh what! I am perfect and proud. . . .
                              Out, deuce! All goes down!
My might and my main are all marring.
Help, fellows! In faith, I am falling.

SECOND FALLEN ANGEL:
From heaven are we hurled down on all hand.
To woe are we wending, I warrant.

LUCIFER THE DEVIL:
Out, out!
Haro, helpless! so hot is it here.
This is a dungeon of dole in which I am dight.
Where are my kin now, so comely and clear?
Now am I loathliest, alas, that ere was so light.
My brightness is blackest of hue now;
My bale is aye beating and burning,
That makes me go grinding and grinning.
Out, ay welaway!
I wallow enough in woe now.

SECOND DEVIL:
Out, out!
I go mad for woe; my wits are all spent now.
All our food is but filth; we swelter in scorn.

We that were builded in bliss, in bale are we burnt now.
Out on thee, Lucifer, lurdan! Our light has thou lorn.
Thy deeds to this dole now have drawn us;
To spoil us thou hast been our speeder,
For thou wast our light and our leader,
Who highest in heaven had called us.

LUCIFER:
Welaway!
Woe is me now; now is it worse than it was.
Uncomfortless carp ye; I said but a thought.

SECOND DEVIL:
Yah, lurdan! You lost us.

LUCIFER:
Ye lie! Out, alas!
I wist not this woe should be wrought.
Out on ye, lurdans; ye smother me in smoke.

SECOND DEVIL:
This woe hast thou wrought us.

LUCIFER:
Ye lie, ye lie!

SECOND DEVIL:
Thou liest, and that shalt abide by.
Here, lurdans; have at ye. Let's look!

ANGEL CHERUBIM:
Ah, Lord,
Loved be thy name, that us this light lent,
Since Lucifer our leader is lighted so low,
For his disobedience in bale to be burnt,
Thy righteousness in right order to show.
Each work even as it is wrought
Through grace of thy merciful might

The cause I see it in sight,
Wherefore into bale he is brought.

GOD:

These fools from their fairness in fantasies fell,
And made nought of might that marked them and made
    them;
Wherefore as their works were in woe shall they dwell;
For some are fallen into filth that evermore shall fade
    them,
And never shall have grace for to shade them.
So passing of power they thought them,
They would not me worship that made them.
Wherefore shall my wrath e'er go with them.
And all that me worship shall dwell here, I wis.
Wherefore in my work go forward I will,
Since their might is marred that meant all amiss,
Even to mine own figure this bliss to fulfil.
Mankind out of mould will I make.
But first before him I create
All things that shall strengthen his state,
To which his own nature shall take.
And in my first making to muster my might,
Since earth is vain void and darkness doth dwell,
I bid by my blessing the angels give light
To the earth, for it faded when fiends fell;
In hell never darkness is missing.
The darkness thus name I for "night,"
And "day" do I call this clear light;
My after works soon shall ye know.
And now in my blessing, I part them in two,
The night from the day, so that they meet never,
But each on its course their gates for to go.
Both the night and the day, do duly your devoir
To all I shall work, without ceasing.
This day's work is done every deal,
And all this work likes me right well,
And straightway I give it my blessing.

THE CREATION OF MAN

York Cardmakers' Play

GOD:

> In heaven and earth the course is seen
> Of five days' work even unto the end,
> I have completed by courses clean;
> Methinks the space of them well spent.
> In heaven are angels fair and bright,
> Stars and planets their course to go;
> The moon serveth unto the night,
> The sun to light the day also.
> In earth are trees and grass to spring,
> Beasts and fowls both great and small,
> Fishes in flood, each other thing . . .
> Thrive they, and have my blessing all.
> And yet can I here no beast see
> That accords by kind and skill,
> And for my works might worship me.
> For perfect work now were it none,
> Save that were made to give it care.
> For love made I this world alone;
> Therefore my love shall there appear.
> To keep this world both more and less
> A skilful beast then will I make
> After my shape and my likeness,
> The which shall worship to me take.
> Of the simplest part of earth that's here
> I shall make man: My motive still,
> For to abate his haughty cheer,

Both his great pride and other ill,
And also to have in his mind
How simple he is at his making,
His feeble state still shall he find
When he shall die, at his ending.
For this reason and cause alone
I shall make man like unto me.
Rise up, thou earth, in blood and bone,
In shape of man, I command thee.
A female shalt thou have for mate,
Whom here I make of thy left side,
That thou alone be not desolate
Without thy faithful friend and bride.
Take ye now here the breath of life,
And receive both your souls of me.
This female take thou to thy wife;
Adam, and Eve, your names shall be.

ADAM:

Ah, Lord, full mickle is thy might,
And that is seen on every side.
For now is here a joyful sight,
To see this world so long and wide.
Many diverse things here now there is,
Of beasts and fowls, both wild and tame,
Yet none is made to thy likeness
But we alone. Ah, loved be thy name.

EVE:

To such a lord in all degree
Be evermore lasting loving,
That to us such a dignity
Has given before all other thing.
And wondrous things may we see here
In all this world so long and broad,
Where beasts and fowls so many appear.
Blessed be he that has us made.

ADAM:

> Ah, blessed Lord, now at thy will,
> Since we are wrought, vouchsafe to tell,
> And also say unto us still,
> What we shall do, and where to dwell.

GOD:

> For this cause made I you this day—
> My name to worship evermore.
> Love me therefore, and love me aye;
> For my making I ask no more.
> Both wise and witty shalt thou be,
> As man that I have made of nought.
> Lordship in earth then grant I thee,
> Each thing to serve thee that is wrought.
> In Paradise ye both shall dwell;
> Of earthly things get ye no need;
> Evil and good both shall ye tell;
> I shall learn you your lives to lead.

ADAM:

> Ah, Lord, since we shall do no thing
> But love thee for thy great goodness,
> We shall obey to thy bidding
> And fulfil it, both more and less.

EVE:

> His sign since he has on us set
> Before all other thing certain,
> Him for to love we will not let,
> And worship him with might and main.

GOD:

> At heaven and earth first I began,
> And six days wrought ere I would rest.
> My work is ended now with man;
> All likes me well, but this the best.

My blessing have they ever and aye.
The seventh day shall my resting be;
Thus will I cease, soothly to say,
Of my doing in this degree.
To bliss I shall you bring;
Come forth, you two, with me;
You shall live in liking.
My blessing with you be.

3

THE GARDEN OF EDEN

York Fullers' Play

GOD:
> Adam and Eve, this is the place
> That I have granted of my grace
> To have your dwelling in.
> Herbs, spices, fruit on tree,
> Beasts, fowls, all that ye see,
> Shall bow to you therein.
> It is called Paradise;
> Here shall your joys begin.
> And if that ye be wise,
> From this need ye never part.
> All your will here shall you have,
> Living for to eat or save
> Flesh, fowl or fish,
> And for to take at your own wish.
> All other creatures at your will,
> Your subjects shall they be.
> Adam, of more and less
> Lordship in earth here grant I thee.
> This place that worthy is,
> Keep it in honesty;
> Look that ye rule it witfully.
> All other creatures shall multiply,
> Each one in tender hour.
> Look then that ye both sow and set
> Herbs and trees, and nothing let,
> So that ye may endeavour

To sustain beast and man
And fowl of each stature.
Dwell here if that ye can;
This shall be your endeavour.

ADAM:

O Lord! loved be thy name.
For this is now a joyful home
That thou has brought us to,
Full of solace calm and mirth,
Herbs and trees and fruit on earth,
With spices many a one, too.
Lo, Eve, now are we brought
To rest and comfort too;
We need to take no thought,
But look all well to do.

EVE:

Loving be aye to such a lord
To us has given so great reward,
To govern both great and small,
And made us after his own mind
(Such pleasure and such play to find)
Amongst the mirths here all.
Here is a joyful sight
Wherein now dwell we shall.
We love thee, most of might,
Great God, on whom we call.

GOD:

Love then my name with good intent
And hearken to my commandment;
My bidding both obey.
Of all the fruit in Paradise
Take ye thereof in your best wise,
And make you right merry.
But the tree of good and ill—
What time you eat of this,
You speed yourselves to spill,

And be brought out of bliss.
All things be made, man, for thy gain;
All creatures bow to thee amain
That here are made earthly.
In earth I make thee lord of all,
And beasts unto thee shall be thrall;
Thy kind shall multiply.
But this one tree alone,
Adam, thus outtake I.
The fruit of it come near none;
For if ye do, ye die.

ADAM:

Ah, Lord, that we should do so ill.
Thy blessed bidding we shall fulfil,
Both in thought and in deed.
We come not nigh this tree nor bough,
Nor yet the fruit that on it grow,
Therewith our flesh to feed.

EVE:

We shall do thy bidding;
We have no other need.
The fruit full still shall hang,
Lord, that thou hast forbid.

GOD:

Look that ye do as ye have said.
Of all that here is hold you glad,
For here is wealth at will.
This tree that bears the Fruit of Life,
Look neither thou nor Eve thy wife
Lay no hands on it still.
Wherefore do my bidding.
It is known both of good and ill;
This fruit save ye let hang,
You speed yourselves to spill.
Wherefore this tree that I outtake,
Now keep it closely for my sake,

That nothing nigh it near.
All other at your will may be;
I outtake nothing but this tree,
To feed you with in fear.
Here shall you lead your life
With dainties that are dear.
Adam, and Eve thy wife,
My blessing have you here.

4

THE FALL OF MAN

York Cowpers' Play

SATAN:
>For woe my wit works wildly here,
>Which moves me mickle in my mind.
>The Godhead that I saw so clear,
>And perceived that he would take kind
>>Of a degree,
>That he had wrought,
>And I denied that angel kind
>>Should it not be.
>For we were fair and bright;
>Therefore methought that he,
>Take one of us he might . . .
>Yet he disdained me.
>The kind of man he thought to take,
>And thereat had I great envy.
>But He has made to him a mate,
>And hard to her I will me hie——
>>That ready way——
>That purpose how to put it by,
>And try to pluck from him that prey.
>My travail were well set,
>Might I him so betray,
>His liking for to let. . . .
>And soon I shall essay.
>In a worm's likeness will I wend,
>And try to feign a likely lie.
>Eve! Eve!

EVE:

> Who is there?

SATAN:

> > I, a friend.
> And for thy good is the coming
> > I hither sought.
> Of all the fruit that ye see hang
> In Paradise, why eat ye not?

EVE:

> We may of them each one
> Take all that we good thought,
> Save one tree out alone,
> Which harms to nigh it ought.

SATAN:

> And why that tree, that would I wit,
> Any more than all other by?

EVE:

> For our Lord God forbids us it,
> The fruit of it, Adam nor I,
> > To nigh it near;
> And if we did, we both should die,
> He said, and cease our solace here.

SATAN:

> Ah, Eve, to me take tent;
> Take heed, and thou shalt hear
> What that same matter meant
> He moved on that manner.
> To eat thereof forbade he you—
> I know it well; this was his skill—
> Because he would none other knew
> Those great virtues that belong to it.
> > For wilt thou see?

Who eats the fruit of good and ill
Shall have knowing as well as he.

EVE:

Why, what kind of thing art thou,
That tells this tale to me?

SATAN:

A worm, that wots well how
That ye may worshipped be.

EVE:

What worship should we win thereby?
We have lordship to make mastery
Of all things that in earth are wrought.

SATAN:

Woman, away!
To greater state ye may be brought,
If ye will do as I shall say.

EVE:

To do we are full loath
Or displease God this way.

SATAN:

Nay, sure; no harm for both;
Eat it safely ye may.
For peril, there none in it lies.
But worship and a great winning;
For right as God shall ye be wise,
And peers to him in everything.
Ay, great gods shall ye be,
Of ill and good to have knowing,
For to be all as wise as he.

EVE:

Is this sooth that thou says?

SATAN:

> Yea; why believe not me?
> I would by no kind of ways
> Tell ought but truth to thee.

EVE:

> Then will I to thy teaching trust,
> And take this fruit unto our food.

SATAN:

> Bite boldly on; be not abashed.
> Give Adam some, to amend his mood
> And eke his bliss.

EVE:

> Adam, have here of fruit full good.

ADAM:

> Alas, woman! Why took thou this?
> Our Lord commanded us both
> To tend this tree of his.
> Thy work will make him wroth;
> Alas, thou hast done amiss.

EVE:

> Nay, Adam, grieve thee nought at it,
> And I shall say thee reason why.
> A worm has given me to wit
> We shall be as gods, thou and I,
>   If that we eat
> Here of this tree. Adam, thereby
> Fail not this worship for to get.
> For we shall be as wise
> As God that is so great,
> And also mickle of price;
> Therefore eat of this meat.

ADAM:

> To eat it would I not eschew,
> Might I be sure in thy saying.

EVE:

> Bite on boldly, for it is true.
> We shall be gods, and know all things.

ADAM:

> To win that name
> I shall it taste at thy teaching.
> Alas! What have I done? For shame!
> Ill counsel! Woe worth thee!
> Ah, Eve, thou art to blame;
> To this enticed thou me.
> My body does me shame,
> For I am naked, as I think.

EVE:

> Alas, Adam, right so am I.

ADAM:

> And for sorrow sore why might we not sink?
> For we have grieved God almighty
> That made me man;
> Broken his bidding bitterly—
> Alas, that ever we began!
> This work, Eve, hast thou wrought,
> And made this bad bargain.

EVE:

> Nay, Adam; blame me not.

ADAM:

> Away, love Eve; who then?

EVE:

> The worm to blame were worthy more;
> With tales untrue he me betrayed.

ADAM:

> Alas, that I list to thy lore,
> Or trusted trifles that you said;
> > So may I bid.
> For I may ban that bitter trade
> And dreary deed that then I did.
> Our shape for dole me grieves.
> Wherewith shall they be hid?

EVE:

> Let us take these figleaves,
> Since it is thus betide.

ADAM:

> Right as thou says so shall it be,
> For we are naked and all bare.
> Full wondrous fain would I hide me
> From my Lord's sight, if I wist where—
> > I care not where.

GOD:

> Adam! Adam!

ADAM:

> > Lord!

GOD:

> > Where art thou,
> > > there?

ADAM:

> I hear thee, Lord, and see thee not.

GOD:

> Say, whereto does it belong,
> This work? Why hast thou wrought?

ADAM:

> Lord, Eve made me do wrong,
> And to this breach has brought.

GOD:

> Say, Eve, why hast thou made thy mate
> Eat fruit I bade thee should hang still,
> And commanded none of it to take?

EVE:

> A worm, Lord, enticed me thereto.
>   So well away!
> That ever I did deed so ill!

GOD:

> Ah, wicked worm! Woe worth thee aye!
> For thou on this manner
> Hast made them such affray.
> My malison have thou here,
> With all the might I may.
> And on thy womb then shalt thou glide,
> And be aye full of enmity
> To all mankind on every side,
> And earth it shall thy sustenance be
>   To eat and drink.
> Adam and Eve, also ye
> In earth now shall ye sweat and swink
>   And travail for your food.

ADAM:

> Alas, when might we sink,
> We that had all world's good?
> Full grievous may we think.

GOD:

> Now, Cherubin, mine angel bright,
> To middle earth swift go drive these two.

ANGEL:

> All ready, Lord, as it is right,
> Since thy will is that it be so
>   And thy liking.
> Adam and Eve, set you to go,
> For here may ye make no dwelling.
> Go ye forth fast to fare.
> Of sorrow may ye sing.

ADAM:

> Alas! For sorrow and care
> Our hands now may we wring.

5

NOAH'S FLOOD

Chester Pageant of the Water-Leaders and Drawers in Dee

> *And first in some high place, or in the clouds if it may be, God speaketh unto Noah standing without the Ark with all his family.*

GOD:

I, God, that all the world have wrought,
Heaven and earth, and all of nought,
I see my people, in deed and thought,
Are set foully in sin.
My spirit shall abide in man,
That through fleshly liking is my foe,
Only till six score years be gone,
To look if he cease from sin.

Man that I made I will destroy,
Beast, worm, and fowl to fly;
For on the earth they do me annoy,
The folk that are thereon.
It harms me so heartfully,
The malice now that can multiply,
That sore it grieveth me inwardly
That ever I made man.

Therefore, Noah, my servant free,
That righteous man art, as I see,
A ship soon thou shalt make thee

45

Of trees dry and light.
Little chambers therein thou make;
And binding-slitch also thou take:
Within and out do thou not slake
To anoint it through all thy might.

Three hundred cubits it shall be long,
And fifty of breadth, to make it strong;
Of height fifty. Do thou with thong
Thus measure it about.
One window work through thy wit,
One cubit of length and breadth make it;
Upon the side a door shall sit,
For to come in and out.

Eating-places thou make also,
Three roofed chambers on a row;
For with water I shall overflow
Man that I did make.
Destroyed all the world shall be,
Save thou; thy wife, thy sons three,
And all their wives also with thee
Shall saved be for thy sake.

NOAH:

Ah, Lord, I thank thee loud and still,
That to me art in such will,
And sparest me and my house to spill,
As now I soothly find.
Thy bidding, Lord, I shall fulfil,
And never more thee grieve nor grill,
That such grace has sent me till
Among all mankind.

To his family:

Have done, you men and women all!
Help, for aught that may befall,
To work this ship, chamber and hall,
As God hath bidden us do.

SHEM:

    Father, I am all ready bound:
    An axe I have, by my crown,
    As sharp as any in all this town,
    For to go thereto.

HAM:

    I have a hatchet wondrous keen
    To bite well, as may be seen;
    A better ground one, as I ween,
    Is not in all this town.

JAPHETH:

    And I can well make a pin,
    And with this hammer knock it in;
    Go and work without more din,
    And I am ready bound.

NOAH'S WIFE:

    And we shall bring timber to,
    For we may nothing else do;
    Women be weak to undergo
    Any great travail.

SHEM'S WIFE:

    Here is a good hackstock;
    On this you may hew and knock;
    Shall none be idle in this flock,
    Nor now may no man fail.

HAM'S WIFE:

    And I will go to gather slitch,
    The ship for to caulk and pitch;
    Anointed it must be every stitch,
    Board, tree and pin.

JAPHETH'S WIFE:

    And I will gather chips here.
    To make a fire for you all here,

And for to make your dinner,
Against you come in.

*Then they make signs as if they were working
with different tools.*

NOAH:

Now, in the name of God, I will begin
To make the ship that we shall in,
That we be ready for to swim
At the coming of the flood.
These boards I join here together,
To keep us safe from the weather,
That we may row both hither and thither,
And safe be from this flood.
Of this tree will I make the mast,
Tied with cables that will last,
With a sail-yard for each blast,
And each thing in their kind;
With topcastle and bowsprit,
With cords and ropes, I have all meet,
To sail forth at the next wet;
This ship is at an end.

Wife, in this castle we shall be kept;
My children and thou, I would, in leapt.

NOAH'S WIFE:

In faith, Noah, I had as lief thou slept.
For all thy frankish fare,
I will not do after thy rede.

NOAH:

Good wife, do now as I thee bid.

NOAH'S WIFE:

By Christ, not ere I see more need,
Though thou stand all the day and stare.

NOAH:

> Lord, that women be crabbed ay,
> And never are meek, that dare I say.
> This is well seen by me to-day,
> As witness you each one.
> Good wife, let be all this clamour
> That thou makes in this place here;
> For all they ween thou art master—
> And so thou art, by St. John!

GOD:

> Noah, take thou thy family,
> And in the ship look that thou hie;
> For none so righteous man to me
> Is now on earth living.
> Of clean beasts with thee thou take
> Seven and seven, ere thou slake;
> He and she, mate to mate,
> Quickly do thou bring.
>
> Of beasts unclean two and two,
> Male and female, and no more;
> Of clean fowls seven also,
> The he and she together;
> Of fowls unclean two and no more,
> As I of beasts said before
> These shall be saved through my love,
> Against I send the weather.
>
> Of all meats that must be eaten
> Into the ship look there be gotten,
> For that no way may be forgotten;
> And do all this right soon,
> To sustain man and beast therein
> Ay till the water cease falling.
> This world is filled full of sin,
> And that is now well seen.

Seven days be yet coming:
You shall have time them in to bring;
After that it is my liking
Mankind for to annoy.
Forty days and forty nights
Rain shall fall for their unrights;
And that I have made through my mights
Now think I to destroy.

NOAH:

Lord, at your bidding I am bain;
Since no other grace will gain,
It will I fulfil fain,
For gracious I thee find.
A hundred winters and twenty
This ship-making tarried have I,
If through amendment any mercy
Would fall unto mankind.

To his family:

Have done, you men and women all!
Hie you lest this water fall,
That each beast were in his stall,
And into the ship brought.
Of clean beasts seven shall be,
Of unclean two; this God bade me.
This flood is nigh, well may we see;
Therefore tarry you nought.

> *Then* NOAH *shall go into the Ark with all his
> family, his wife except, and the Ark must be
> boarded round about, and on the boards all the
> beasts and fowls hereafter rehearsed must be
> painted, that these words may agree with the
> pictures.*

SHEM:

Sir, here are lions, leopards in,
Horses, mares, oxen, and swine;

Goats, calves, sheep, and kine
Here sitten thou may see.

HAM:

Camels, asses men may find,
Buck, doe, hart, and hind;
And beasts of all manner kind
Here be, as thinketh me.

JAPHETH:

Take here cats and dogs too,
Otter, fox, skunk also;
Hares hopping gaily can go
Have cabbage here to eat.

NOAH'S WIFE:

And here are bears, wolves set,
Apes, owls, marmoset,
Weasels, squirrels, and ferret;
Here they eat their meat.

SHEM'S WIFE:

Yet more beasts are in this house:
Here cats make it full carouse;
Here a rat and here a mouse,
They stand nigh together.

HAM'S WIFE:

And here are fowls, less and more:
Herons, cranes, and bittor,
Swans, peacocks; and them before
Meat for this weather.

JAPHETH'S WIFE:

Here are cocks, kites, crows,
Rooks, ravens, many rows,
Ducks, curlews, whoever knows
Each one in his kind;
And here are doves, ducks, drakes,

Redshanks running through the lakes;
And each fowl that singing makes
In this ship men may find.

NOAH:

Wife, come in! Why stands thou there?
Thou art ever froward, that dare I swear.
Come in, for God's sake! Time it were,
For fear lest that we drown.

NOAH'S WIFE:

Yea, sir, set up your sail,
And row forth with evil hail,
For, without any fail,
I will not out of this town
If I have not my gossips every one,
One foot further I will not gone;
They shall not drown, by St. John,
If I may save their life.
They loved me full well, by Christ,
Unless thou let them in thy chest,
Else row forth, Noah, whither thou list,
And get thee a new wife.

NOAH:

Shem, son, lo! thy mother is wroth:
Such another I do not know, forsooth.

SHEM:

I shall fetch her in, by my troth,
Without any fail.

He goes to his mother.

Mother, my father after thee sent,
And bids thee into yonder ship wend.
Look up and see the wind,
For we be ready to sail.

NOAH'S WIFE:

> Son, go again to him, and say
> I will not come therein to-day.

NOAH:

> Come in, wife, in twenty devils' way,
> Or else stand there without.

HAM:

> Shall we all fetch her in?

NOAH:

> Yea, sons, in Christ's blessing and mine;
> I would you hied you betime,
> For of this flood I am in doubt.

GOSSIP: (*to Wife*)

> The flood comes fleeting in full fast,
> On every side it spreads full far;
> For fear of drowning I am aghast;
> Good gossip, let us draw near.
>
> And let us drink ere we depart,
> For oft-times we have done so;
> For at a draught thou drink'st a quart
> And so will I do ere I go.

NOAH'S WIFE:

> Here is a pottle of Malmsey, good and strong;
> It will rejoice both heart and tongue;
> Though Noah thinks us never so long,
> Yet we will drink alike.

JAPHETH:

> Mother, we pray you altogether—
> For we are here your own childer—
> Come into the ship for fear of the weather,
> For his love that you bought!

NOAH'S WIFE:

> That will I not, for all your call,
> But I have my gossips all.

SHEM:

> In faith, mother, yet you shall,
> Whether you will or nought.

> *Then they carry her in.*

NOAH:

> Welcome, wife, into this boat.

NOAH'S WIFE:

> And have thou that for thy note!

> *She boxes him on the ear.*

NOAH:

> Aha! marry, this is hot!
> It is good to be still.
> Ah, children, methinks my boat removes;
> Our tarrying here hugely me grieves.
> Over the land the water spreads;
> God do as he will!

> Ah, great God that art so good,
> He that works not thy will is wood.
> Now all this world is on a flood,
> As I will see in sight.
> This window will I shut anon,
> And into my chamber will I be gone,
> Till this water, so great an one,
> Be slaked though thy might.

> *Then NOAH shall shut the window of the Ark,
> and for a little space within board he shall be
> silent, and afterwards opening the window and
> looking round about, saying:*

Now forty days are fully gone,
Send a raven I will anon,
If aught-where earth, tree, or stone
Be dry in any place;
This betokeneth God has done us some grace,
And is a sign of peace.
Ah, Lord, honoured must thou be!
All earth drys now, I see;
But yet, till thou command me,
Hence will I not hie.
All this water is away;
Therefore, as soon as I may,
Sacrifice I shall do, in fay,
To thee devoutly.

GOD:

Noah, take thy wife anon,
And thy children every one;
Out of the ship thou shalt be gone,
And they all with thee.
Beasts and all that can fly
Out anon they shall hie,
On earth to grow and multiply;
I will that it so be.

NOAH:

Lord, I thank thee through thy might;
Thy bidding shall be done in hight,
And as fast as I may dight
I will do thee honour,
And to thee offer sacrifice;
Therefore come, in all wise,
For of these beasts that be his,
Offer I will this store.

> *Then going out of the Ark with all his family*
> *he shall take his animals and birds and offer*
> *them in sacrifice.*

Lord God in majesty,
That such grace has granted me,
Where all was lorn, safe to be,
Therefore now am I bound,
My wife, my children, and family,
With sacrifice to honour thee;
Of beasts, fowls, as thou mayst see,
I offer here right soon.

GOD:

Noah, to me thou art full able,
And thy sacrifice acceptable;
For I have found thee true and stable,
On thee now must I mind:
I will curse the earth no more
For man's sin that grieves me sore;
For from his youth man full yore
Has been inclined to sin.

A covenant, Noah, with thee I make,
And all thy seed for thy sake,
Of such vengeance for to slake,
For now I have my will.
Here I give my promise fast
That man, woman, fowl nor beast,
With water, while the world shall last,
I will no more spill.

My bow between you and me
In the firmament shall be,
By very token that you may see
That such vengeance shall cease,
That man nor woman never more
Be wasted by water, as is before;
But for sin that grieveth me sore,
Therefore this vengeance was.

When clouds are in the heavenly sphere
That same bow shall then appear

In token that my fierce anger
Shall no more vengeance take
The string is turned toward you,
And toward me is bent the bow,
That such weather shall never show;
And this promise I make.

My blessing now I give thee here,
To thee, Noah, my servant dear,
For vengeance shall no more appear;
And now farewell, my darling dear.

6

THE SACRIFICE OF ISAAC

Brome Manuscript

ANGEL:

>Abraham's heart will God now assay,
>Whether that he be steadfast or wild;
>His good will to God now show he may,
>If he loveth God more than his child.

ABRAHAM:

>Father of heaven omnipotent,
>>With all mine heart to thee I call;
>Thou has given me both land and rent,
>And my livelihood thou hast me sent;
>>I thank thee highly ever of all.
>First of the earth thou madest Adam,
>>And Eve also to be his wife;
>All other creatures of them two came,
>And now thou grantest me, Abraham,
>>Here in this land to lead my life.
>In my old age thou hast given me the bliss
>>To have a young child, a darling one.
>I love nothing so much, I wis,
>Except thyself, dear Father of bliss,
>>As Isaac, that is mine own sweet son.
>And, therefore, Father of heaven, I thee pray
>For his health and also for his grace;
>Now, Lord, keep him both night and day,

That never trouble nor evil affray
    Come to my child in no place.

ANGEL:

Abraham, Abraham, cease thy request.
    Our Lord commandeth thee for to take
Isaac, thy young son that thou lovest best,
    And with his blood sacrifice that thou make.

ABRAHAM:

I had rather, if God had so willed,
    Have given up all the goods that I have
Than that Isaac my son should be killed,
    As God in heaven my soul may save!

I never loved anything so much on earth,
    And now I must the child go kill.
Against thee my conscience is sorely stirred,
    . . . And yet, my dear Lord, I am sore afeard
    To grudge anything against your will.

I love my child as my life;
    But yet I love my God much more.
For though my heart would fain make strife,
Yet will I not spare for child nor wife,
    But do all things after my God's lore.

ANGEL:

Abraham, Abraham, this is well said.
    I shall thee lead to a mountain high.
Now in thy heart be nothing dismayed.

ABRAHAM:

Nay, nay, forsooth, I hold me well arrayed
    To please my God to the best that I may.
Isaac, Isaac, mine own son dear,
    Where art thou, child? Speak to me.

ISAAC:

My father, sweet father I am here,
Making my prayers to God's majesty.

ABRAHAM:

Rise up, my child, and fast come hither,
My gentle son that art so wise,
For we two straight must go together
And unto the Lord make sacrifice.
Hold this faggot upon thy back,
And here myself fire shall bring.

ISAAC:

Father, all this here will I pack,
I am full eager to do your bidding.

ABRAHAM:

Ah, Lord of heaven! my hands I wring;
These words hurt me more than anything.
Now, Isaac son, go we our way
Unto yon mount with all our main.

ISAAC:

Go we, dear father, as fast as we may;
To follow you I am full fain,
Although I be slender.

ABRAHAM:

Ah, Lord, my heart breaketh in twain,
This child's words be so tender.
Now, Isaac, son, anon let it down;
No longer upon thy back it hold;
For now I must make ready soon
To honour my Lord God as I should.

ISAAC:

Lo, my dear father, where it is.
To cheer you always I draw me near.

But father, I marvel sore at this,
 That thou dost make such heavy cheer.
And also, father, something dread I:
 Where is the live beast you should kill?
Fire and wood we have both ready,
 But no beast have we on this hill.
A living beast, I know well, must die
 Your sacrifice to God for to make.

ABRAHAM:

 Dread thee nought, my child, say I;
  Our Lord will send me one for to take.

ISAAC:

 Yea, father, but my heart quaketh so;
  To see your sharp sword drawn I wonder.

ABRAHAM:

 Ah, Father of heaven! So am I woe,
  This child doth break my heart in sunder.

ISAAC:

 Tell me, my dear father, if you please,
  Have ye your sword drawn for me?

ABRAHAM:

 Ah, Isaac, my son, peace, peace!
  For thou dost break my heart in three.

ISAAC:

 I pray you, father, let me hear
  Whether I shall have any harm or no.

ABRAHAM:

 Sweet son, to tell thee I cannot bear;
  My heart was never so full of woe.

ISAAC:

 Dear father, I pray you hide it not away,
  But some of your thought now tell me.

ABRAHAM:

Ah, Isaac, Isaac, I must thee slay.

ISAAC:

What have I done, alas! that ye should kill me?
If I have trespassed against you in aught,
With a rod ye may beat me till I be full mild,
And with your sharp sword kill me not,
For I wis, father, I am but a child.

ABRAHAM:

I am full sorry, son, thy blood for to spill,
But truly, child, I may not choose.

ISAAC:

I would to God my mother were on this hill;
She would plead for me on both her knees,
To save my life.
But since my mother is not here,
I pray you, father, change your cheer
And kill me not with your knife.

ABRAHAM:

Forsooth, son, if I do not this deed,
Greatly displeasèd our Lord will be.

ISAAC:

Nay, nay, then, father, God forbid
That ever ye should grieve him for me.
Ye have other children one or two
Whom ye should love well by kind;
I pray you now, father, make no ado,
For, once I be dead, and from you go,
I shall be soon out of your mind.
Therefore do ye our Lord's bidding,
And when I am dead, then pray for me.
But, father, tell ye my mother nothing;
Say that I am in a far country dwelling.

ABRAHAM:

Ah, Isaac, Isaac, blest may thou be!
My heart beginneth now to gainsay
To shed the blood of thy blessed body.

ISAAC:

Father, it may be no other way;
Let death pass over me speedily.
But, father, before I go to my death,
I pray you bless me with your hand.

ABRAHAM:

Now, Isaac, with all my breath,
My blessing I give thee upon this land.
And God's also, I wis.
Now, fairest son, up thou stand,
Thy mouth that I may kiss.

ISAAC:

Fare thee well, my own father so fine.
Greet my mother with cheerful word.
I pray you, father, to hide my eyne,
That they see not the stroke of your sword,
That my flesh shall defile.

ABRAHAM:

Son, thy words make me weep full sore;
Wherefore I pray thee speak no more.

ISAAC:

We shall speak together but a while.

ABRAHAM:

Ah, God, give me strength to do thy will!
Ah, Isaac, mine own sweet child!
Yet kiss me again upon this hill.
In all this world is none so mild.

ISAAC:

Now truly, father, all this tarrying
    It doth my heart but harm;
I pray you, father, make an ending.

ABRAHAM:

    Come up, sweet son, under my arm.
I must bind thy hands too,
    Though thou be never so mild.

ISAAC:

Mercy, father, why should ye so?

ABRAHAM:

    Lest thou shouldst struggle, my child.

ISAAC:

Nay, father, I will not hinder you,
    But let you do after God's will,
And after the purpose ye have set you;
    For God's love keep on with it still.
But, father, I pray you once more,
    None of this to my mother tell.
For if she knew, she would weep full sore;
    For I wis, father, she loved me full well.
        Now farewell, my mother so sweet!
        We two be like no more to meet.
Sweet father, I am sorry to grieve you.
    I cry you mercy of this I have done,
And of all trespass I ever did against you;
    Forgive me, father, before God's throne.
        God of heaven be with me!

ABRAHAM:

Ah, dear child, leave off thy moans;
    In thy life thou hast grieved me but this once;
Now blessed be thou, body and bones,
    And God ever be with thee!

And now, dear son, here shalt thou lie.
  Unto my work I must me steel.
I wis I had liefer myself to die,
  If but it had pleased God as well,
    And mine own body to offer.

ISAAC:

  Ah, mercy, father, mourn ye no more;
  Your weeping maketh my heart as sore
    As mine own death that I shall suffer.

ABRAHAM:

  Now farewell, child so full of grace.

ISAAC:

  Ah, father, father, turn downward my face,
    For your sharp sword I dread surely.
  Ah, Father of heaven, to thee I cry:
    Lord, receive me into your hand.

ABRAHAM:

  Lo, now is the time come certain
    That my sword in his neck shall bite.
  Ah, Lord, mine heart riseth there again,
    And suffereth me not to smite;
      I cannot strike the blow.
  Great God, fain would I work thy will;
  But this young innocent lieth so still—

ISAAC:

  Alas, father, haste me to kill;
    Why dost thou tarry so?

ABRAHAM:

  Now, heart, if thou wilt not break in three,
  I will no longer stay for thee,
  For that my God grieved would be.
    Now, child, receive the blow.

He raiseth his sword to strike, which the ANGEL, *suddenly appearing, taketh in his hand.*

ANGEL:

Abraham, Abraham, thy hand hold.
From heaven to thee am I sent.
Our Lord thanketh thee an hundred-fold
For the keeping of his commandment.
He knoweth thy will and also thy heart,
That thou dreadest him above all thing;
And that thy heaviness now may depart,
A fair ram yonder did I bring.
Now farewell, blessed Abraham;
Make thy sacrifice with yon ram,
And spare thy son so free.

ISAAC:

Ah, mercy, father, why smite ye not yet?
Smite on, father, at once with your knife.

ABRAHAM: (*untying him*)

Peace, my sweet son, and up thou get,
For our Lord of heaven hath granted thy life
By his angel now,
That thou shalt not die this day, son, truly.

ISAAC:

Ah, father, full glad then were I—
I wis, father—I say—I wis—
If this tale were true.

ABRAHAM:

An hundred times, my son fair of hue,
For joy I would thee kiss.

ISAAC:

But, my dear father, Abraham,
Will not God be wroth that we do thus?

ABRAHAM:

> Nay, nay, truly, my sweet son,
> For he hath sent a propitiation
>> Hither down to us;
> Yon beast shall die here in thy stead,
>> In the worship of our Lord alone.
> Go, fetch him hither, my child, indeed.

ISAAC:

> I shall go bind him feet and head
>> And bring him with me anon.

ABRAHAM:

> Now be right merry, my sweet child,
> For that same beast that is so mild
>> I shall present before all other.

ISAAC:

> Lo, father, this ram to you I give:
> I thank thee, Lord, that I shall live
>> And kiss once my sweet mother.
> Now will I fast begin to blow;
>> This fire shall burn a full good speed.
> But father, when I stoop down low
>> Kill me not with thy sword indeed!

ABRAHAM:

> Nay, son, be thou relieved;
>> My mourning is past.

ISAAC:

> But I would the sword were sheathed;
>> It maketh me aghast.

ABRAHAM:

> Almighty God omnipotent,
>> My offering I make before thy face,
> And with this beast I thee present,
>> As thou art God and ground of our grace.

ANGEL:

> Abraham, Abraham, well may thou speed,
>> And Isaac, thy young son thee by;
> Truly, Abraham, for this deed,
> God shall multiply both your seed
>> As thick as stars in sky.
> Of your seed shall come the Greatest One
>> That ever is in bliss without end;
> For that ye serve God with perfect awe
> And even to death ye keep his law,
>> Himself to your seed he shall lend.

ABRAHAM:

> Lo, Isaac my son, how think ye
>> Of this work that we have wrought?
> Full glad and blithe may we be,
>> That against God's will we rebelled not,
>> Upon this heath.

ISAAC:

> Ah, father, I thank our Lord full well
> That my wit served me so well
>> To dread God more than my death.

ABRAHAM:

> Come on with me, my own sweet son,
>> And homeward fast let us roam.

ISAAC:

> By my faith, father, thereto I am one—
>> I was never so glad to go home
>> And to speak with my dear mother.

ABRAHAM:

> Ah, Lord of heaven, I thank thee,
> For now I may lead home with me
> Isaac, my young son so free,
>> Gentle above all other.

ANGEL:

    Good Christian people, these that ye have seen
      Are foreshadowers of Jesu's sacrifice,
    Bearing the woes of earth most keen,
      Without gainsaying, in God's service.
    So Christians all that sorrow borne
      And kept God's word without a miss,
    Jesu, that wore the crown of thorn,
      Bring them all to heaven's bliss.

7

I. DAVID TAKES THE SHOOTS
TO JERUSALEM

Cornish: The Legend of the Rood

And KING DAVID *shall perform, and he shall parade.*

DAVID:
> After talk and work
> It would be a good plan
> To take drink and food,
> And after that rest.
> Butler, make haste,
> Bring me the best wine,
> Sleep slips upon me
> And drowsihead.

BUTLER:
> Dear King David, be not angry;
> Whether you shall be thirsty or hungry,
> Wherever I may be, as soon as I hear you,
> I come.
>
> Parlez, vous êtes seigneur mien,
> For any better drink of wine
> Slips not down thy throat;
> In this country is no better,
> Nay, my lord, there is no liquor
> Equal to this wine of note.

DAVID:

> Blessing upon thee, butler!
> The drink is sweet and clear,
> By God of Heaven.
> And now I will sleep;
> Sleep is heavy upon me,
> O wondrous heavy.

COUNSELLOR:

> Lie down, lie down, my lord;
> You shall be covered
> With richest array,
> Becoming a king of your degree.

GOD:

> Gabriel, great Angel,
> To Jerusalem go;
> Say to King David,
> He will find in Mount Tabor,
> In arid Arabia,
> Rods planted by Moses.

> Let him bring them to Jerusalem,
> For there shall be born in Bethlehem
> A son to redeem the world.
> Out of them they will make a cross
> To crucify Christ, my darling Son;
> Happy he who shall worship him.

GABRIEL:

> O Father, as thou art full of grace,
> I will do all as thou wilt;
> Thy command in every place
> Shall be fulfilled.

> *And then he shall come to* KING DAVID, *he being alone.*

GABRIEL:

David, to arid Arabia go,
To the mountain of Tabor;
Take thence three rods
Which were planted by Moses,
And carry them home again,
Back to Jerusalem.
Mankind will have need of them,
For the day will surely come
To make a fateful cross of them.

Then the king, waking up, says marvelling:

DAVID:

Lord, you say well!
I have seen in my dream
The bright Angel Gabriel;
He told me to bring,
For the salvation of all men,
The rods from Mount Tabor.

Herald, bring my horse here
Forthwith to ride;
All my household shall come,
Both commons and knights.

HERALD:

My lord, by God's day,
The gay steed is ready,
And the bay courser,
And charger and palfrey
In fairest array.
Lord, mount when thou wilt.

DAVID:

Herald, all thanks for thy heed.
Come, let us set forward
On our long journey.
And that well we may speed,

Let us pray God to guide
Us in his mercy.

Here let KING DAVID *come down.*

In the name of God
I mount my steed;
Over my soul
May his spirit guard.

Then he shall ride.

Blessed be the time
When the angel told me.
Behold we are come
To the mountain of Tabor.

Alight, every mother's son.
See the rods before us,
Growing so green.
In high honour to God
From the ground I will cut
These rods of grace.

COUNSELLOR:

Those indeed are rods of grace,
For you have not smelt in any place
Fragrance like this ever.
God himself is in this hill,
Now I feel and know full well,
So sweet is their savour.

DAVID:

Strike tabors, play minstrels,
Three hundred harps and trumpets,
Dulcimer, fiddle, viol and psaltery,
Shawms, lutes and kettle-drums,
Cymbals, organs and recorders,
In sweet symphony.

Now let us remount
In the name of the Father,

And hasten back home,
Knight and squire together.

BLIND MAN:

Dear Lord David, help me
With your rods as you ride;
Blind I am, I cannot see;
Let them prove my guide.

LAME MAN:

To me also, the maimed man,
Give power to go firm,
And that they are rods of greatest grace
I will affirm.

DAVID:

You shall be cured if you believe
The grace of the rods has power to heal.
In the name of Father, Son and Holy Ghost,
Each of you shall now be whole.

BLIND MAN:

All praise, for God the Father of Heaven
Has heard and answered our desire,
And healed us each of our disease
By virtue of these peerless rods.

Here let him alight from horseback.

DAVID:

Now are we home, and here dismount.
But before we go to the palace,
Tell me, where shall these rods be planted,
That they may flourish and most be honoured?

COUNSELLOR:

My lord, while I consider this,
Let them lie upon the grass,
Appointing guards to watch them.

DAVID:

In faith, I will follow thine advice.
Butler and herald, I command you
To watch them with the greatest care
On pain of hanging and drawing.

And now I will rest before I eat,
For I am tired and needs must sleep.

KING DAVID *goes up into his tent.*

HERALD:

I will keep them with great honour;
The strongest man in all the world,
Though he be a king or kaiser,
Shall not take them from this place.

BUTLER:

Nor king nor emperor nor sultan,
However mighty, shall remove them;
Safely in Jerusalem
I will keep the rods of grace.

HERALD:

Butler, lie on one side
And watch and listen every way;
If any fellow filch them—

BUTLER:

By my belt, he shall not bag them
Be he never so boasting a braggart,
Or big of his body,
So sleep on thy belly and rest.
Or if thou wilt have a wench,
I will bring thee a beauty.

Then the king, waking from sleep, says:

DAVID:

Softly have I rested;
How sweet is the morning sleep!
Honoured be God the Father
In his work always.
That I may have grace,
I will go to plant
The rods with care
In some fair place.

HERALD:

Pray reconsider your plan, my lord,
For a wondrous thing has happened this night;
The rods are rooted in the earth,
And all the three are joined in one.

DAVID:

Worship to the Lord of Heaven,
For all his works are wonderful.

He shall go to the rods.

Since he has planted them in this place,
Here they shall stay.
And that the tree may have high honour,
Let there be made a circlet of silver
To measure its girth.

BUTLER:

I have one here of purest silver
To circle it. Now we may see
How much the tree shall grow each year.

II. DAVID AND BATHSHEBA

Cornish: The Legend of the Rood

> And KING DAVID *says to* BATHSHEBA, *washing her
> dress in the stream:*

DAVID:

Lady, in thy gentleness,
I beseech thee, love me;
Never have I seen a woman
Pleases me above thee.

Thou shalt have my palaces,
All my halls and chambers;
Be my love and live with me,
And I thy lover ever.

BATHSHEBA:

Dear my lord, to be thy love
Would be thy lady's pleasure,
Were she but free from marriage vows,
To live with thee for ever.

Let BATHSHEBA *go home with* KING DAVID.

DAVID:

Bathsheba, rose of all the world,
Our loves enclose thy husband's life;
He shall not defeat our joy,
And thou shalt be King David's wife.

BATHSHEBA:

Dear David lord, thy lady lays thee
Open all her precious treasure;
But either he or I must die
Should he discover us together.

DAVID:

God made of thee, my dearest heart,
The fairest flower in his garden;
Thy husband shall not live to part
The harvest from the harvester.

DAVID:

Sir Uriah, my trusted knight,
A fearful foe is in the land.
I am so sick I cannot go,
So pray thee take a host well armed,
And put this enemy to flight.

URIAH:

My heart rejoices at thy news,
And leaps, my lord, to learn thy will;
Either thine enemy shall die,
Or I myself will not return.

DAVID:

I like thine answer well, sir knight,
Our country cannot boast thy peer;
But in the battle look thou lead
The van to prove thou hast no fear.

URIAH:

No taunt of cowardice shall taint
My honour, good my lord;
I shall be the first to strike
Blows with my sword.
Farewell, I will no longer stay,
But, sire, in going, bless me, I pray.

DAVID:

Uriah, my blessing on thee,
Mayst thou never come to harm.
My butler and my herald
Shall support thee with their arm.

URIAH:

Before I depart
I must see my wife;
To leave without word
Would break her heart.

He speaks to BATHSHEBA:

Sweet Bathsheba, I must leave thee
In battle to labour.
But do not grieve; I shall return,
And maybe the end will not be long.

Here URIAH *is prepared and armed.*

BATHSHEBA:

O dear my lord, you must not talk so,
My heart would break if you should go;
If you should go, and forsake my bed,
Nevermore will I taste bread.

URIAH:

My Bathsheba, my faithful wife,
I must go at the king's command.
One kiss more before I leave,
Then pray for me, my life, my love.

He kisses her and goes. Here URIAH *comes down.*

BATHSHEBA:

Alas, that ever I was born!
I shall faint for sorrow.
Every eve and morrow
Will I pray that thou return—
Never!

Here GABRIEL *comes down.*

URIAH:

Here, herald, carry my banner
Before me to battle;
And thou, butler, follow with valour,
As thou lookest for honour.

Here he mounts a horse.

HERALD:

> My lord, thou canst rely on me;
> I shall be with thee in victory.

> *And then they shall ride out of the stage. And*
> *afterwards the* HERALD *comes, and says to* KING
> DAVID:

> All hail, great king!
> Behold me come again home;
> But grievous news I bring.
> Sir Uriah is killed in battle,
> And with him thy butler.

DAVID:

> What! Sir Uriah is dead!
> How shall I be comforted?
> Tell me, as thou lovest me,
> When death took him, and how he died,
> For he was stout and valiant,
> Confident in strength and pride.

HERALD:

> Yet cold he is as any stone.
> He strove to break the foeman's ranks,
> But a trooper drove him to the ground,
> And pierced and hacked him to the bone.

> *Then the* ANGEL *shall come to* KING DAVID, *and ask*
> *him a question; and he says:*

GABRIEL:

> Answer me, thou mighty king.
> If a man who had a hundred sheep,
> And his neighbour only one,
> Then should steal the poor man's lamb,
> What punishment is due to him?
> Answer me, thou mighty king.

DAVID:

Certainly I will answer thee.
The man who did this thing should die,
And should restore the lamb fourfold,
Because he did this pitiless thing.

KING DAVID *comes down.*

GABRIEL:

Thou art the man.
Thou hast killed Uriah with the sword,
And taken his wife to be thy wife.
Therefore thy wives shall be taken
And given to thy neighbour;
And the sword shall never depart from thine house.

DAVID:

I have sinned against the Lord
With the body of this wicked woman.
Lord, pardon my soul. Have mercy
Upon me according to thy pity,
And, sitting beneath the tree of grace,
I will begin a psalm of praise.

*And then, under the Tree of Knowledge, he begins
the Psalter, namely, "Beatus vir":*

Blessed is the man that walketh
Not in the counsel of the ungodly,
Nor standeth in the way of sinners,
Nor sitteth in the seat of the scornful.
But his delight is in the law of the Lord,
And in his law doth he meditate
Day and night. And he shall be like a tree
Planted by the rivers of water,
That bringeth forth his fruit in his season;
His leaf shall not wither,
And whatsoever he doeth shall prosper.

My sweet adviser, I pray thee,

Teach me some atonement
For my transgression. What shall I do
To appease the blessed Father?

COUNSELLOR:

In atonement for thy sins,
Order the building of a temple,
Beautiful and ample;
Summon the masons of the city,
And proclaim it to the people.

DAVID:

The blessing of God be on thee,
For surely this is good advice.
I will take thy counsel in all things.

KING DAVID *goes up.*

Herald, my servant, command
All the masons to assemble
Here tomorrow,
On pain of hanging without pity,
To make a wall of noble stones
In the centre of the city.
In honour of God,
Here will I build a temple.

HERALD:

My lord, I go to do thy command.

DAVID:

Fare thee well, my faithful herald.
Drink a draught of mead or wine
To make thee nimble in thine errand.

Here God the Father comes down.

HERALD:

Oyez! All masons, listen to me!
On pain of hanging and drawing,

Take care to be tomorrow morning
In the centre of the city,
There to build a noble temple.

> *And he shall come again to the king, and he says
> to him:*

Lord David, I have warned the masons
Great and small;
Tomorrow early will they come
To build the wall.

DAVID:

Herald, I grant thee
Reward for thy service:
For Carnsew and Trehembys
Thyself make a charter.

HERALD:

Worthy lord, gramercy;
Thy presents are princely.

FIRST MASON:

Thou lad, make ready lime and clay,
Stones, sledge-hammers and wedges;
And I will hasten within
To build the walls and ledges.

SECOND MASON:

The foundations are finished already,
But there will be trouble unless we hurry.

DAVID:

Counsellor, let us go and see
How well the masons do their work;
If any dare to scamp or shirk,
Dire punishment shall be their fee.

> *Here he goes down.*

COUNSELLOR:

> The finest craftsmen in the land
> You shall find working at your command.

Let God be in the plain.

GOD:

> David, thou shalt not build my house;
> Unworthy the man who has killed a man.
> Thou hast destroyed an image of my face,
> Thou shalt not make my temple.

DAVID:

> Lord, who then shall build it?

GOD:

> Solomon, thy son, shall make my temple.

Here God goes up.

DAVID:

> Now I know my end is come.
> I have lived a long time.

DAVID *shall go to the tents.*

> My lords, I pray you,
> Crown Solomon, my son.
> As ye have honoured me,
> So honour him.
> God has appointed him,
> Therefore anoint ye him,
> Blow with the trumpet, saying,
> God save King Solomon.

HERALD:

> My lord, thy will shall be done,
> As it behoves me in all things.

DAVID:

    Dear God, praise to him, will not grant me
    Leave to live any longer in error.
    O God, in thy hands lift up my soul;
    Preserve it from terror.

    And then KING DAVID *shall die.*

COUNSELLOR:

    Alas! alas! King David is dead:
    Now indeed is a time to grieve.
    Let us pray to God to receive his soul,
    And bury his body in the grave.

    *And he shall bury him, and carry the body under
    some tent.*

8

THE PARLIAMENT OF HEAVEN:
THE ANNUNCIATION AND CONCEPTION

Hegge Cycle

CONTEMPLATION:
Since Adam and Eve by the serpent fell,
   Man for his offence and foul folly
Hath lain in Limbo, as I you tell,
   And were worthy to lie therein endlessly.
     But then should perish your great mercy,
       Good Lord; have on man pity,
     Have mind of your prayer said by Isaye,*
     Let mercy meek be thine highest majesty.

Would God thou would'st break thine heaven mighty
   And come down here to earth indeed,
And live therein years three and thirty,
   Thy famished folk with thy food to feed;
   To staunch their thirst let Thy side bleed.
     For else will not be made redemption.
Come visit us in this time of need,
     On Thy careful creatures have compassion.

Ah, woe to us! Wretches of wretches we;
   For God hath added sorrow to sorrow.
I pray Thee, Lord, Thy souls come see,
   How they lie and sob both even and morrow.

* Isaiah.

With Thy blessed blood from bales them borrow—
   Thy careful creatures crying in captivity.
Ah, tarry not, gracious Lord, till it be morrow,
   Lest the devil take man by his iniquity.

O waters, give to mine eyes such rain
   That I may weep both day and night,
To see our brethren in so long pain;
   Their mischiefs amend by Thy much might.
     As great as the sea, Lord, now is Satan's might;
     From our head is fallen the crown;
Man is covered in sin; I cry to Thy sight:
     Gracious Lord, gracious Lord, gracious Lord, come
      down.

(The Parliament of Heaven.)

Enter MERCY, JUSTICE, TRUTH *and* PEACE. JUSTICE
and TRUTH *seat themselves.*

TRUTH:
Lord, I am Thy daughter Truth,
   That shall last without an end.
And I must testify to man's ruth,
   That wretch was to Thee so unkind.
     Thy holy will he did abjure;
     Thou art his creator and he is Thy creature,
     Thou hast loved Truth, it is said evermore,
     Therefore in pains let him evermore endure.

MERCY:
O Father of mercy and God of comfort,
   Who counsellest us in each tribulation,
Let your daughter Mercy to you resort,
   And on man misled have Thou compassion.
     Him grieveth full greatly his transgression;
     All heaven and earth cry for mercy;
     Meseemeth that none should take exception
      Their prayers have been offered so specially.

JUSTICE:
Mercy, me marvelleth what you moveth;
  You know well I am your sister Justice.
God is rightful and righteousness loveth;
  Man offended Him that is endless,
    Therefore his endless punishment may never cease;
      Also he forsook his maker that made him of clay,
And the devil to be his master he chose.
    Should he be saved? Nay, Nay, Nay.

MERCY:
Sister Justice, ye are too vengeful.
  Endless sin God endless may restore.
Above all His works God is merciful.
  That he forsook God, man always doth deplore;
  And though he presumèd never so sore,
    Yet must thou consider the frailness of mankind.
Learn an ye list, this is Godès lore:
    The mercy of God is without an end.

PEACE:
To spare your speeches, sisters, it were fit;
  It is not honest in Virtues to be in dissension.
The Peace of God overcometh all wit;
  Though Truth and Justice say great reason,
  Yet Mercy saith best to my pleasing.
    For if man's soul should abide in hell,
  Between God and man ever should be division;
    And therein might not I, Peace, dwell.

Therefore meseemeth best ye thus accord,
  Lest heaven and earth ye should divide:
Put both your sentences unto our Lord,
    And in His high wisdom let Him decide.

TRUTH: (*rises*)
In truth hereto I consent,
  I would pray our Lord so it might be.

JUSTICE: *(rises)*
I, Justice, am well content,
  For in Him is very equity.

MERCY:
And I, Mercy, from His counsel will not flee,
  Till Wisdom shall have said I shall cease.

PEACE:
Here is God now, here is unity;
  Heaven and earth are pleased with Peace.

  They hold up hands of supplication. GABRIEL *appears.*

GABRIEL:
This is Godès word, you shall confess.
  Adam died once for his transgression,
That truth and also righteousness
  Might be preserved from violation.
    Now to restore mercy and peace,
      A second Adam must die on earth;
So Godès mercy to man shall not cease,
And the reign of peace shall come to birth.

But he that shall die, ye must know
  That in him be none iniquity,
That hell may hold him by no law,
  But that he may pass at his liberty.

  Find therefore the man that is worthy
    His death for man's death to be redemption.
  All heaven and earth seek now ye,
    That our Lord may fulfil His intention.

  TRUTH, JUSTICE *and* MERCY *search and return.*

TRUTH:
I, Truth, have sought the earth without and within,
  And in sooth there can none be found

That is of human birth without sin,
  Nor that to death will be bound.

MERCY:

I, Mercy, have run the heavenly region round,
  And there is none of that charity
That for man will suffer a deadly wound.
  I cannot tell how this shall be.

JUSTICE:

Sure I can find none sufficient,
  For servants unprofitable we be each one;
His love needeth to be full ardent
  That for man to hell would be gone.

PEACE:

None is there but one that can this do.
  Therefore this is Peace's advice,
That we beseech God to give Himself thereto;
  For the conclusion in Him of all this lies.

> *They kneel and pray. After a time the* VOICE OF GOD
> *is heard; all the* VIRTUES *and* GABRIEL *prostrate them-*
> *selves.*

VOICE OF THE FATHER:

From us, God, angel Gabriel, thou shalt be sent
  Into the country of Galilee;
To a city called Nazareth be thine intent,
  To a maid. Betrothed to a man is she
  Of whom the name is Joseph, he
    Of the house of David born.
  The name of the maid free
    Is Mary, of Joachim born.

VOICE OF THE SON:

Say that she is without sin and full of grace,
  And that I, the Son of the Godhead, son shall be to her.
Hie thee, that thou arrive apace,

Else we shall before thee be there.
I have so great haste to be made man
In that meekest and pure virgin,
That I may bring to naught what Satan began,
Of all you angels and of men the great ruin.

VOICE OF THE HOLY GHOST:
And if she ask thee how it may be,
Tell her that I, the Holy Ghost, shall work all this.
She shall be overshadowed by our Unity.
In token whereof, her cousin Elizabeth is
Quick with child in her great age, I wis;
For to Us there is nothing impossible.
Her body shall be so filled with bliss
That soon shall she think these tidings credible.

GABRIEL: (*rising*)
In thine high embassy, Lord, I shall go
More speedily than it may be thought.
Behold now, Lord, I go hereto,
I take my flight and bide nought.

The VIRTUES *rise and embrace.*

PEACE:
Now is the loveday made of us four finally,
And we may live in peace as we did formerly,
Mercy and Truth are met together;
Justice and Peace have kissed each other.

They depart, singing "Mercy and Truth are met together, etc." (Psalm 85).

MARY:
Lord, seven petitions I beseech of you here;
First that I may keep Thy love and Thy law,
The second to love my neighbour as myself dear,
The third, from all that Thou hatest me to withdraw,
The fourth, to do all things that Thou wouldest have done

The fifth, to obey the rulers of Thy temple each one,
The sixth, that all people may serve Thee with awe,
   That in Thy holy family fault be none.

The seventh, Lord, I ask with great fear:
   That I may see once in my life
That lady that shall Godès Son bear,
   That I may serve her with my wits five.
     If it please you and with your will doth not strive,
      With prayers prostrate for these graces I weep;
     O my God, devotion deep in me drive,
      That my heart may wake in Thee though my body
       sleep.

GABRIEL:

Ave Maria, gratia plena, dominus tecum.
   Hail, full of grace, God is with thee,
   Above all women blessed art thou.

MARY:

Ah, mercy God, this is a marvellous hearing;
   In the angel's words I am troubled here.
I wonder what manner is this of greeting;
    And also thus highly commended to be
   I am most unworthy; I cannot answer,
    Great awe and a mighty dread is on me.

GABRIEL:

Mary, in this take ye no dread,
   For you have found grace with God almighty.
Ye shall conceive in your womb indeed
   A child, the second person of the Trinity.
   His name of you JESUS shall be called,
    He shall be great, above every sovereign;
   And on his father David's throne shall be installed,
    Over the house of Jacob endlessly to reign.

MARY:

Angel, I say to you,
  In what manner of wise shall this be?
For no man do I know;
  I have evermore kept my virginity.

GABRIEL:

The Holy Ghost shall come from above to thee,
  And the virtue of the highest o'ershadow thee so.
Therefore that holy child that shall be born of thee,
    As Son of God shall all people do him homage.
For witness whereof, your cousin Elizabeth, she
    Hath conceived a son in her old age.
    This is the sixth month of her childbearing,
    Whom to call barren none was sparing.

Mary, come off and haste thee,
  And take heed, thou dear,
How the Holy Ghost, blessed He be,
  Is waiting for thine answer.
Furthermore, all the blessed spirits of virtue
  That are in heaven before Godès face,
And all the good livers and true
  That are here in this earthly place
  And the chosen souls this time of grace
That in Limbo are waiting for rescue,
As Adam and Eve, David and Isaiah,
  And many other of good reputation,
All these thine answer desire to hear,
  And thine assent to the Incarnation,
In which thou standest as preserver
  Of all mankind's salvation.
Give me mine answer now, lady dear,
  To all these creatures' comfortation.

MARY:

With thy gracious bidding I myself accord,
  Bowing down my face with all benignity:
See here the handmaiden of our Lord,
  After thy will be it done to me.

GABRIEL: (*kneels*)
Gramercy, lady free,
  Gramercy of your answer full right,
Gramercy of your great humility,
  Gramercy, ye lantern of light.

> *Here the* HOLY GHOST *descendeth with three beams to
> our lady; the son of the Godhead next with three
> beams to the* HOLY GHOST; *the* FATHER GODLY *with
> three beams to the* SON; *and so enter all three to her
> bosom.*

MARY:

Ah, now I feel you in my body be,
  Perfect God and perfect Man,
You take not first one member and then another,
  But perfect childhood ye have anon.

Of your handmaiden now have you made your mother,
  Without pain, in flesh and bone.
  Thus conceived never woman none
    That ever was in this life.
  O my highest Father on your throne,
    It is meet that your Son, now my Son, have a pre-
    rogative.

GABRIEL:

Now farewell, turtle, Godès daughter dear,
  Fare thee well, Godès mother, I do thee honour.
Farewell, Godès playfellow and His sister,
  Fare thee well, Godès chamber and His bower.

MARY:

Farewell, Gabriel, Godès messenger express.
I thank you for your travel and your goodness.
  I pray you that ye would in your faring
    Make it an accustomed occupation
  To visit me often in my childbearing;
    Your presence is my sweetest comfortation.

GABRIEL:

At your will, lady, so shall it be,
House of the Godhead, so of homage worthy.
I commend me unto you, thou throne of the Trinity,
    O meekest maid, now the mother of Jesu;
    And as I began, I end, with an AVE new
      Enjoined upon heaven and earth. With that, I leave
        you.

9

THE BIRTH OF CHRIST

York Tile-Thatchers' Play

JOSEPH:
All wielding God in Trinity,
I pray thee, Lord, for thy great might,
Unto thy simple servant see,
Here in this place where we are pight,
    Ourselves alone.
Lord, grant us good harbour this night
    Where we have gone.
For we have sought both up and down,
Through divers streets in this city;
So much people is come to town,
That we can nowhere harboured be,
    There is such press.
Forsooth I can no succour see
    But shelter with the beasts.
And if we here all night abide,
We shall be stormed here in this stead;
The walls are down on every side,
The roof is ruined above our head,
    As I may rue.
Say, Mary, daughter, where is thy rede?
    How shall we do?
For in great need now are we stead,
As thou thyself in sooth mayest see;
For here is neither clothes nor bed,
And we are weak and all weary,
    And fain would rest.

Now, gracious God, for thy mercy
      Guide us the best.

MARY:

God will us guide, full well wit ye;
Therefore, Joseph, be of good cheer.
For in this place born will he be
That shall save us from sorrows here
      Both even and morn.
Sir, wit ye well the time is near
      He will be born.

JOSEPH:

Then it behoves us bide here still,
Here in this same place all this night.

MARY:

Yea, sir; forsooth it is God's will.

JOSEPH:

Then would I fain we had some light,
      What so befall.
It wakes right dark unto my sight,
      And cold withal.
I will go get us light this tide,
And fuel find with me to bring.

MARY:

All wielding God you govern and guide,
As he is sovereign of all thing,
      For his great might,
And lend me grace to his loving
      To wait aright.
Now in my soul great joy have I;
I am all clad in comfort clear.
Now will be born of my body
Both God and man together here.
      Blest might he be!
Jesus! My son that is so dear,

Now born is he.
Hail, my Lord God! Hail, prince of peace!
Hail, my father, and hail, my son!
Hail, sovereign strong all sins to cease!
Hail, God and man on earth in one!
Hail, through whose might
All this world was first begun,
Darkness and light!
Son, as I am simple subject of thine,
Vouchsafe, sweet son, I pray to thee,
That I might take thee in these arms of mine,
And in this poor weed array thee.
Grant me thy bliss,
As I am thy mother chosen to be
In truthfulness.

JOSEPH:

Ah, Lord, what! The weather is cold,
The fellest freeze that e'er I did feel.
I pray God help them that is old,
Or find it till their limbs to wield;
So may I say.
Now, good God, be thou my shield.
As thou best may.
Ah, Lord God! What light is this
That comes shining thus suddenly?
I cannot say, as I have bliss.
When I come home unto Mary,
I will ask her.
Ah, here be good, for here come I.

MARY:

You are welcome, sir.

JOSEPH:
Say, Mary daughter, what cheer with thee?

MARY:
Right good, Joseph, as has been aye,

JOSEPH:

    Oh, Mary—what sweet thing is that on thy knee?

MARY:

    It is my son, the sooth to say,
        So mild of mood.

JOSEPH:

    Well is me I did bide this day
        To see this good.
    I marvel mickle of this light,
    That thuswise shineth in this place;
    Forsooth it is a wondrous sight.

MARY:

    This has he ordained of his grace,
        My son so young,
    A star to be shining a space
        At his bearing.
    For Balaam told full long before,
    How that a star should rise full high,
    And of a maiden should be born
    A son that shall our saving be
        From cares so keen.
    Forsooth it is my son so free
        Balaam did mean.

JOSEPH:

    Now welcome, flower fairest of hue,
    I worship thee with main and might.
    Hail, my Maker! Hail, Christ Jesu!
    Hail, royal king, root of all right!
        Hail, Saviour!
    Hail, my Lord, gleaming so light!
        Hail, blessed flower!

MARY:

    Now, Lord, that all this world shall win,
    To thee, my son, is what I say.

Here is no bed to lay thee in,
Therefore, my dear son, I thee pray,
    Since it is so,
Here in this crib I might thee lay
    Between these beasts two.
And I shall hap thee, mine own dear child,
With such poor clothes as we have here.

JOSEPH:

O Mary, behold these beasts so mild!
They make loving in their manner,
    As they were men;
Forsooth it seems well by their cheer,
    Their lord they ken.

MARY:

Their lord they ken, that wot I well;
They worship him with might and main.
The weather is cold, as ye may feel;
To hold him warm they are full fain
    With their warm breath,
And breathe on him, it is certain,
    To warm him with.
Now sleeps my son, blest might he be,
And lies full warm these beasts between.

JOSEPH:

O now is fulfilled, forsooth I see
What Habakkuk in mind did mean,
    And preached by prophecy;
He said our Saviour shall be seen,
    Between beasts lie.
And now I see the same in sight.

MARY:

Yea, sir; forsooth the same is he.

JOSEPH:

Honour and worship both day and night
Aye—lasting lord, be done to thee
    All way as is worthy.
Lord, to thy service I bind me,
    With all my heart wholly.

MARY:

Thou merciful Maker, most mighty,
My God, my Lord, my son so free,
Thy handmaiden forsooth am I,
And to thy service I bind me
    With all my heart entire.
Thy blessing, so beseech I thee,
    Thou grant us all now here.

10

THE PLAY OF THE SHEPHERDS

Wakefield Cycle: Secunda Pastorum

COLL:
Lord, but these weathers are cold and I am ill happed.
My hands cannot hold, so long have I napped.
My legs bend and fold, my fingers are chapped.
It is not as I would, for I am all lapped
In sorrow.
In storms and tempest,
Now in the east, now in the west,
Woe is him has never rest
Midday nor morrow.

But we silly shepherds that walk on the moor,
In faith, we are near turned out of the door;
No wonder, as it stands, if, we be poor
For the tilth of our lands lies fallow as the floor,
As ye ken.
We're so burdened and tanned,
Overtaxed and unmanned,
We're made tame to the hand
Of these gentlery men.

For they take all we have—Our Lady them weary!
These lordings so brave, they make the plough tarry,
That men say is for the best—we find it contrary.
Thus are husbandmen opprest, in point to miscarry
On life.

Thus hold they us under,
Thus they bring us in blunder,
It were a great wonder
  If ever we should thrive.

There cometh a swain as proud as a peacock,
He must borrow my wain, my plough and my stock;
Try I with might and main I must grant ere he go.
Thus live we in pain, anger and woe,
  By night and day.
He must never be flouted,
Though I must do without it:
I'll be hanged, never doubt it,
  If I once say him nay.

It does me good, as I walk thus by my lone,
Of this world for to talk in manner of moan.
To my sheep will I stalk, and hearken anon,
There abide on a balk, or sit on a stone
  Full soon,
For I trow, perdie,
True men if they be,
We get more companie
  Ere it be noon.

GIB:
"Beniste" and "Dominus," what may this mean?
Why, fares the world thus oft have we not seen?
Lord, these weathers are spitous and the winds full keen
And the frosts so hideous they water mine een,
  No lie.
Now in dry, now in wet,
Now in snow, now in sleet,
When my shoes freeze to my feet,
  It is not all easy.

But as far as I ken or yet as I go,
We silly wedded men suffer most woe;

We have sorrow then and then—it falls out so:
Look at Capel our hen! both to and fro
   She cackles:
But begin she to croak,
To groan or to cluck,
Woe is him our cock—
   He is in the shackles.

But now late in their lives, a marvel to me,
That I think my heart rives such wonders to see,
But where destiny drives it so shall be—
Some men will have two wives and some men three
   In store!
Some are woe that has any,
But on this I'll bet a penny,
Woe is him that has many,
   For he feels sore!

But young men a-wooing, for God that you bought,
Be ware well of wedding, and think in your thought
"Had I known" is a saying that profits you naught.
A great deal of mourning has marrying bought
   And griefs,
With many a sharp shower;
For thou mayst catch in an hour
That shall savour full sour
   As long as thou lives.

For, as I read epistle, I have one at my fire
As sharp as a thistle, as rough as a briar,
She is browed like a bristle, with eyes full of ire,
When she once wets her whistle she can outsing the choir
   At pater-noster.
She is as great as a whale,
She has a gallon of gall:
By him that died for us all
   I would I had run till I lost her.

COLL:

Gib, look over the row! Art as deaf as a post?
The devil in thy maw—thou are not lost.
Saw ye aught now of Daw?

COLL:

 Yea, on the highland
Heard I him blow: he comes near at hand
 I declare
Stand still now.

GIB:

 And why?

COLL:

For he cometh, hope I:
Let us hide us hereby
 And give him a scare.

DAW:

Christ's cross me speed and Saint Nicholas!
Thereof have I need, it is worse than it was,
I scarce keep my feet on the snow and the ice,
I am ever in dread—it is as brittle as glass
 And slithers.
This world fared never so sore
Since the great flood of Noah.
With tempests more and more
 And everything withers.

We that walk in the nights our cattle to keep
We see sudden sights when other men sleep.
 Sees others.
Yet me thinks my heart lights: I see shrews peep.
Ye are two wicked wights that will give my sheep
 A turn.
But full ill have I meant;

As I walk on this bent
I may lightly repent
 My toes if I spurn.

Ah, sir, God you save—and master mine!
A drink fain would I have and something to dine.

GIB:
Christ's curse, my knave, thou art a lazy hind!

COLL:
What, the boy will rave: the belly's whine
 Him teases.

GIB:
Ill thrift on thy pate!
Though the shrew came late
Yet is he in state
 To dine when he pleases.

DAW:
Such servants as I that sweat long and toil
Eat our bread full dry, and that makes me boil.
We are oft wet and weary when master-man winks,
Yet is he niggardly with dinners and drinks;
 And alway
Both our dame and our sire,
When we have run in the mire,
Know how to dock our hire
 And put off our pay-day.
  To GIB
But hear my plan, master:—for the fare that you give
I shall do thereafter—work as I receive
I shall do a little, sir, and then take my leave—
For ne'er does your supper my stomach relieve
 In the fields.
Where to should I weep
When away I can leap?

A servant hired cheap
Cheap work yields.

COLL:
Thou were an ill lad to go on serving
A man that has but little for spending.

GIB:
Peace, boy, I bade, no more jangling,
Or I shall make thee afraid, by the Heaven's king,
    With thy gauds.
Where are our sheep in this storm?

DAW:
Sir, this same day at morn
I left them in the corn
    When they rang lauds.

They have pasture good, they cannot go wrong.

GIB:
That is right! By the rood these nights are long!
Yet I would, ere we go, one would give us a song.

COLL:
So I thought, as I stood, for mirth us among.

DAW:
    I grant.

COLL:
Let me sing the tenory.

DAW:
And I the treble so high.

GIB:
Then the mean falls to me.
    Let's see how ye chant.

They sing. Enter MAK.

MAK:

Now Lord, for thy names seven, that madest the moon
And stars I cannot reckon, give thy help as my boon.
Distraught I am driven, my brain flyeth wild.
Would God I were in Heaven, for there weeps no child
    Without cease.

COLL:

Who is this that pipes so poor?

MAK:

Would God ye knew what I bore!

COLL:

Lo, a man that walks on the moor
    And has not all his ease!

GIB:

Mak, what news ere thou came? Tell us the tidings.

DAW:

Is he come? Then each one take heed to his things.

Takes MAK'S *cloak from him.*

MAK:

What? I am a yeoman, I tell you, of the king's
Sent expressly in his name to some great lordings
    And such people.
Fie on you! Go hence
Out of my presence:
I must have reverence
    And stand high as a steeple.

GIB:

Mak, the devil in your ee! A stroke would I lend you.

COLL:

Mak, know ye not me? By God, I could skin you!

MAK:

God bless you all three, I thought that I knew you!
Ye're a fair company, 'tis a pleasure to meet you.

DAW:

That's steep!
And thus late as thou came,
Ye'll get a bad name,
For you have an ill fame
  For stealing of sheep.

MAK:

And I true as steel as all men know!
But a sickness I feel that holds me full low,
With pain I could squeal, 'tis as sharp as a goad.

DAW:

Seldom lies the deil dead by the road.

MAK:

  Therefore
Full sore am I and ill,
I've not eaten what will
Go on point of a needle
  This month or more.

COLL:

How's thy wife? by my hood, how doth her life go?

MAK:

Lies lolling, by the rood, by the fire, lo!
And a house full of brood. She drinks well too;
There is no other good that she will do
  But so:
Eats as fast as she can,
And each year that comes to man

She brings forth a bairn,
  And some years two.

So were I more gracious and richer by far
I were eaten out of house and of harbour.
She is lazy as a louse, and if ye come near
She has ever a grouse, so that I live in fear
  Of her tongue.
Will ye see what I proffer?
To give all in my coffer
Tomorrow morn to offer
  Her requiem sung.

GIB:
I wot that so weary is none in this shire.
I must sleep, though he's leery, this boy that I hire.

DAW:
I am frozen and weary and would have a fire.

COLL:
My eyes are all bleary, I'm like to expire:

  To GIB

Wake thou!

GIB:
Nay, we must trust the boy
On the sheep to cast an eye.

DAW:
As good a man's son was I
  As any of you.

  GIB *and* COLL *sleep.*

But Mak, come hither and lie between them two.

MAK:
And thus may I gather what they whisper so low.
Pater noster—Our Father—*qui es in caelo*—

DAW *watches.*

About me, lad, don't bother, but go to sleep so,
  Have no dread.

  DAW *sleeps.*

From my top to my toe
In manus tuas commendo,
Pontio Pilato!
  Sees DAW *watching: crosses himself.*
Christ's cross me speed.

  DAW *sleeps:* MAK *makes sure, then rises.*

Now's the time for a man whose platter is cold
To stalk secretly as he can into a fold,
And nimbly to plan, nor be too bold,
Or he'll rue the bargain when it be told
  At the ending.
Now were time for to revel;
But he needs good counsel
That fain would fare well
  And has but little spending.

  Draws a magic circle.

But about you a circle as round as a moon,
Till I've done what I will, till that it be noon,
That ye lie stone still till I have done;
And I shall say theretill of good words a rune.

  Mutters.

  On height
Over your heads my hand I lift,
Out go your eyes, fordo your sight.
But yet I must make better shift
  Ere it be right.

  SHEPHERDS *snore.*

Lord! what they sleep hard! that may you all hear;
Was I never a shepherd, but to learn I've no fear.

If the flock be scared yet will I slip near.
See, my dears, come hitherward! Now mends our cheer
  From sorrow.

    He has a sheep.

A fat sheep, I dare say,
A good fleece, I dare lay!
When I can I'll repay,
  But this will I borrow.

    He takes sheep home.

How, Gill, art thou in? Get us some light.

GILL:
Who makes such a din this time of the night?
I am set for to spin; I hope not I might
Rise a penny to win—beshrew thee on height!
  So fares
A poor wife with your quirk.
To be roused doth me irk:
I never can do any work
  For such small chares.

MAK:
Good wife, open quick: don't you see what I bring?

GILL:
Do thou draw the sneck. (*Sees sheep*) Ah, come in, my
      sweeting.

MAK:
Yea, thou didst not reck of my long standing.

GILL:
By thy naked neck thou art like for to hang.

MAK:
  Get away!
I am worthy my meat,

For in a strait can I get
More than they that swink and sweat
　　All the long day.

Thus it fell to my lot, Gill, I had such grace.

GILL:
It were a foul blot to be hanged for the case.

MAK:
I have often got out from as tight a place.

GILL:
But "so long goes the pot to the water," men says,
　　"At last
"Comes it home broken."

MAK:
Well I know the token,
But let it never be spoken;
　　Come and help fast.

I wish he were slain, I list well eat:
This year was I not so fain of any sheep-meat!

GILL:
Come they ere he be slain and hear the sheep bleat—

MAK:
Then might I be ta'en—that were a cold sweat.
　　Go bar
The gate-door.

GILL:
　　Yes, but, Mak,
If they come at thy back—

MAK:
Then might I be, for all the pack,
The devil of the war.

GILL:

A good trick have I spied, since thou canst think of none.
Here shall we him hide till they be gone—
In my cradle abide! Let me alone,
And I shall lie beside in sickbed and groan.

MAK:

Get ready!
And I shall say thou wast light
Of a man-child this night.

GILL:

Now is the day bright
That ever I was bred.

This is a good guise and a fair cast:
Yet a woman's advise helps at the last!
Lest anyone spies, go back again fast.

MAK:

Come I not ere they will rise it will blow a cold blast.
I will go sleep!

MAK *goes back to field.*

Still sleep all this crew,
And I will stalk in too,
As if I never knew
Who carried their sheep.

Lies down and snores: COLL *wakes.*

COLL:

Resurrex a mortuis! Have hold my hand!
Judas carnis dominus! I may not well stand:
My foot sleeps, by Jesus, and I parched as sand.
Methought that we laid us full near England.

GIB:

Ayee!
Lord, but I have slept weel;

As fresh as an eel,
As light I me feel
  As leaf on a tree.

DAW:

Blessing be herein! So my body quakes,
My heart is out of my skin and my limbs shake.
Who makes all this din? So my head aches,
To the door will I win. Hark, fellows, wake!
  We were four.
See ye ought of Mak now?

COLL:

We were up ere thou.

GIB:

Man, I give God a vow
  He has stayed on the floor.

DAW:

Methought he was lapped in a wolf-skin.

COLL:

So are many wrapped now, only within.

DAW:

When we had long napped, methought with a gin
A fat sheep he trapped, but he made no din.

GIB:

  Be still!
Thy dream makes thee mad,
'Tis but phantom, my lad.

COLL:

God make us all glad,
  If it be his will!

GIB:

Rise, Mak, for shame, thou liest right long.

MAK *yawns and rises.*

MAK:
Now Christ's holy name be us among,
What is this, by Saint James? I can scarce get along.
I hope I am the same. Ah, my neck has lain wrong
  And quaint!
Many thanks. Since yestreen
Now, by Saint Stephen,
I was flayed with a dream
  Made my heart to faint.

I thought Gill began to croak and travail full sad
Almost at the first cock, of a young lad
For to mend our flock; then be I never glad.
I have trouble in stock more than ever I had.
  Ah, my head!
A house full of young bairns—
The devil knock out their brains!
Woe is him has many bairns
  And thereto little bread!

I must go home, by your leave, to Gill as I thought.
I pray you look in my sleeve, that I steal naught.
I am loth you to grieve or from you take ought.

DAW:
Don't try to deceive! (*Drives* MAK *off*) Now I would that
      we sought
  This morn
That we had all our store.

COLL:
But I will go before.
Let us meet.

DAW:
            Where?

GIB:
  At the crooked thorn.

Exeunt. MAK *at home.*

MAK:

Unbar the door, do: you're asleep, I suppose.
You have nothing to do but play with your toes.

GILL:

Why, who wanders, who wakes, who comes, who goes?
Who brews, who bakes, who makes me these hose?
  And my man,
It is sad to behold,
Now in hot, not in cold,
Full woeful is the household
  That wants a woman.

But what end has thou made with these shepherds, Mak?

MAK:

The last word that they said, when I turned my back,
They would look that they had their sheep all the pack.
I know they'll be mad to find one of them lack,
  Perdie!
And I fear me these boys
Will not follow my decoys
But will make a foul noise
  And cry out upon me.

Come, save me, my mate!

GILL:

  I accord me theretill.
I shall swaddle him right in my cradyll.
In any such fight I'll help with a will.
I will lie down straight. Tuck me up, then.

MAK:

                                                I will.

GILL:
Behind!
These shepherds will burrow
And search us full narrow.

MAK:
But I'll cry 'Out, harrow!'
    The sheep if they find.

GILL:
Hearken ay for their call—they will come anon.
Come and make ready all and sing on your own,
Sing 'lullay' thou shall, for I must groan
And cry out by the wall on Mary and John
    Full sore.
Sing lullay on fast,
When thou hears them at last:
And but I play as I'm cast
    Trust me no more.

The SHEPHERDS *reassemble.*

DAW:
Ah, Coll, good morn, why smilest thou not?

COLL:
Alas, that ever I was born! We have a foul blot:
A fat sheep have we lorn.

DAW:
                        Marry, God forbott!

GIB:
Who should do us that scorn and so cunningly plot?

COLL:
    Some shrew.
I have sought with my dogs
All Horbury Shrogs

And with the fifteen hogs
  Found I but one ewe.

DAW:

Now trow me, if ye will, by Saint Thomas of Kent,
Either Mak or Gill was in that argument.

COLL:

Peace, man, be still, I saw when he went;
Thou slanders him ill, thou ought to repent
  Good speed.

DAW:

Now swear I to thee,
If I should even here die,
I would say it were he,
  That did that same deed.

GIB:

Go we thither, I rede, and run on our feet;
I shall never eat bread the truth till I wit;

COLL:

Nor drink in my head with him till I meet.

DAW:

I will rest in no bed till that I him greet
  My brother.

GIB:

My troth here I plight
Till I see him in sight
Shall I never sleep one night
  Where I do another.

They approach MAK's *house.*

DAW:

Will ye hear how they squawk? Our sir tries to croon.

COLL:

Heard I never none crack so clear out of tune.
Call on him.

GIB:

Mak, undo, your door soon.

MAK:

Who is it that spake as if it were noon
  Aloft?
Who is that, I say?

DAW:

Good fellows, were it day.

MAK:

As far as ye may,
  Good sirs, speak soft.

Over a sick woman's bed that lies full of woes,
I had rather be dead than she had more sorrows.

GILL:

Get away from my bed, and walk on your toes,
Each step that you tread goes clean through my nose.
  So—hee!

COLL:

Tell us, Mak, if ye may,
How fare ye, I say?

MAK:

Glad you're in town today.
  Now how fare ye?

Ye have run in the mire and are dripping wet.
I will make you a fire if ye will sit
And give drink and food: methinks that ye sweat.

GIB:
Nay, neither mends our mood, drink nor meat.

MAK:
What's the matter?

DAW:
Someone stole our best sheep.
It touches us deep.

MAK:
Had I not been asleep
I'd have made his teeth chatter.

GIB:
Mak, here is one avows that it should be ye.

DAW:
Either you or your spouse, so say we.

MAK:
If your doubts we arouse, either Gill or me,
Come and search our house, and then may ye see
Who had her—
If I any sheep got,
Or cow or what-not:
And Gill my wife rose not
Here since we laid her.

As I am true and leal, to God I here pray
That this be the first meal I shall eat this day.

Indicate Sheep.

COLL:
Mak, if thou needs heaven's weal, take care now: they say
"He learned early to steal that could not say nay."

The shepherds search, GILL *shams faintness.*

GILL:
  I swelt!
Out, thieves, from my old bones.
You come to rob us. Oh!

GIB:

                    She moans.

MAK:
Hear ye not how she groans?
  Your hearts should melt.

GILL:
Out, thieves, from my bairn: nigh him not near!

MAK:
Wist ye how she had fared your hearts would be sore.
Ye do wrong, I you warn that thus come before
To a woman that hath fared—but I say no more.

GILL:
  Ah, my middle!
I pray to God so mild
If ever I you beguiled
That I eat this child
  That lies in this cradle.

MAK:
Peace, Woman, for God's pain, and cry not so!
Thou spillest thy brain and makest me full of woe.

GIB:
I think our sheep is slain, what think ye two?

COLL:
We work all in vain, we may as well go.
  But, hatters,
I can find no flesh,

Salt nor fresh,
Nor any dish
  But two empty platters.

No cattle but this, tame nor wild,
None, so may I come to bliss.

DAW:

                              Too soon have you smiled!

GILL:
No, so God give me bliss and joy of my child.

COLL:
We have worked amiss, I hold us beguiled.

GIB:
  Sir, done!
Sir, our lady give him joy,
Is your child a boy?

MAK:
Any lord might enjoy
  This child for his son.

GIB:
Mak, friends will we be, for now we're at one.

MAK:
Yet for your slight on me amends get I none.

    Taking hand.

Farewell, all three, (*aside*) and glad ye were gone.

DAW:
Fair words there may be, but love there is none
  This year.
Gave ye the child anything?

They leave MAK's *house.*

GIB:
I trow, not a farthing.

DAW:
Fast again will I fling—
   Wait for me here.

   DAW *returns.*
Mak, take it not ill if I come to thy bairn.

MAK:
Nay, thou hast a will to do me some harm.

DAW:
The child I'll not grieve, that little day-starn;
Mak, with your leave, let me give your bairn
   But sixpence.

MAK:
Nay, go away, he sleeps.

DAW:
Methinks he peeps.

MAK:
If he wakes he weeps,
   I pray you go hence.

   The other shepherds return.

DAW:
Give me leave him to kiss, and lift up the clout.
What the devil is this? He has a long snout.

COLL:
He is marked all amiss, we wait ill about.

GIB:

Ill spun woof, I wis, alway cometh foul out.
  Ay, so!
He is like to our sheep.

COLL:

How, Gib, may I peep?

    MAK *and* GILL *try to escape.*

DAW:

I see thieves will creep
  Where they may not go.

GIB:

This was cunningly wrought, I ne'er saw it surpassed.

COLL:

It was a huge fraud.

DAW:

                    Yea, sirs, was't.
Let us tie up this bawd and bind her fast.
A false scold when she's caught hangs at the last.
  So shalt thou.
Will ye see how they swaddled
His four feet in the middle?
Saw I never in cradle
  A horned lad ere now.

I know him be the ear-mark, this is a good token.

MAK:

I tell you, sirs, hark! His nose was broken;
I was told by a clerk he was under a spell.

COLL:

This is a false work: I would fain ring his knell:
  Get weapon.

GILL:
He was changed by an elf,
I saw it myself,
When the clock struck twelve
    Was he mis-shapen.

GIB:
You two are right deft at spending your breath.

COLL:
Since they maintain their theft let us do them to death.

MAK:
To your mercy I'm left: if I'm not a changed man
Of my head I'll be bereft.

DAW:
                          Masters, hear my plan:
    For this trespass
Let us neither kill nor fight,
Curse nor chide,
But seize him tight
    And cast him in canvas.

They toss MAK. *He and* GILL *creep away.*

COLL:
Lord, but I am sore, at point for to burst
I can go no more but must have a rest.

GIB:
As a sheep of seven score he weighed in my fist.
To sleep anywhere methinks I am pressed.

DAW:
    Now I pray you
Some sleep let us get.

COLL:
On those thieves think I yet.

DAW:
Wherefore should ye fret?
  Do as I say you.

They sleep. An angel appears.

ANGEL:
Rise, shepherds, have joy, for now is he born
That shall take from the fiend what Adam had lorn;
That fiend to destroy this night is he born.
God is made your friend; and you on this morn
  He behests:
To Bethlehem go see,
There lies that baby
In a crib full poorly
  Beside two beasts.

GLORIA *is sung.*

COLL:
This was a quaint stave as ever I heard,
It is a marvel to name and I am afeard.

DAW:
Of God's son he gave from Heaven a word:
On the fields shone a flame that like lightning he made
  Appear.
He spoke of a bairn
In Bethlehem, I you warn.

COLL:
That betokens yonder starn:
  Let us seek him there.

GIB:

Say, what was his song? Heard ye not how he cracked it?
Three breves to a long.

DAW:

                    Yea, marry, he hacked it:
Was no crochet wrong, nor nothing that lacked it.

GIB:

For to sing us among, right as he knacked it.
  I can.

COLL:

Let us hear how ye croon;
Can ye bark at the moon?

GIB:

Hold your tongue, have done:
  Hark after, then.

   He sings and fails: they laugh.

COLL:

To Bethlehem he bade us that we should go along;
I am full afraid we tarry too long.

DAW:

Be merry and not sad, for a journey we're strong,
Everlasting glad, without needing a song
  To upstay us.

COLL:

Hie we thither quickly,
Though we be wet and weary,
To see that child and that lady
  Let nothing delay us.

GIB:

We find by the prophecy—let be your din—
Of David and Isaye and more as I mean
They prophesied by clergy that in a virgin
Should he light and lie to soften our sin
 And slake it,
To catch our kind from woe.
For Isaye said so:
Ecce Virgo
 Concipiet a child that is naked.

DAW:

Full glad may we be, and remember the day
That lovely to see, that all mights may.
Lord, well it were for me, if once and for aye
I might kneel on my knee, some word for to say
 To that child.
But the angel said
He was poorly arrayed,
And in a crib was laid
 Among beasts wild.

COLL:

Patriarchs that have been, and prophets beforn,
They desired to have seen this child that is born—
They are gone away clean, that have they lorn.
We shall see him, I ween, ere it be morn,
 To token.
When I see him and feel
Then know I full weel
It is true as steel
 That prophets have spoken.

To so poor as we are that he would appear,
First find and declare by his messenger.

GIB:

Go we now, let us fare, the place is us near.

DAW:

I am ready and yare, go we in fear
  To that bright.

DAW:

Lord, if thy will it be
We are lewd all three,
Thou grant us of thy glee
  To comfort thy wight.

They approach the Crib.

COLL:

Hail, comely and clean, hail, young child!
Thou wast born of a queen among maidens—he smiled!
Thou hast scared him, I ween, that old Satan so wild,
The deceiver so mean himself is beguiled.
  Lo, he merrys!
Lo, he laughs, my sweeting!
A well-fare meeting!
Here's my proper greeting—
  Have a bob of cherries?

GIB:

Hail, sovereign Saviour, for thou hast us bought,
Hail freely, leaf and flower of all that men sought,
Hail, full of favour, that made all of nought,
Hail, I kneel and I cower! A bird have I brought
  To my bairn.
Hail, tiny little mop!
Of our creed thou art the prop,
I would drink in thy cup,
  Little day-starn.

DAW:

Hail, darling dear, full of godheed!
I pray thee be near when that I have need.
Hail, sweet is thy cheer! My heart doth bleed

To see thee sit here in so poor weed
   With no pennies.
Hail, put forth thy dall:
I bring thee but a ball;
Have and play thee withal
   And go to the tennis.

MARY:
The father of night, God omnipotent,
That set all things alight, his Son hath us lent:
I conceived him forthright, through his Ghost as he meant:
He came forth as light through glass that is sent,
   And now is he born.
He keep you from woe—
I shall pray him do so.
Tell his praise as ye go
   And mind on this morn.

COLL:
Farewell, lady so fair to behold,
With thy child on thy knee.

GIB:
                        But he lies full cold.

Wraps his cloak round child.

Now well is me, and we go, thou behold.

DAW:
For sooth, all ready it seems to be told
   Full oft.

COLL:
What grace have we found!

GIB:
Now are we safe and sound.

DAW:
To sing are we bound:
　Make it echo aloft!

　　Exeunt singing.

11

HEROD AND THE KINGS

Coventry Shearmen and Tailors' Play

HERALD:
Peace, lord barons of great renown,
Peace, seigneur knights of noble order,
Peace, gentlemen companions of eminence,
I command all of you keep silence.
Peace while your noble king is in presence;
Let no one stint to pay him deference,
For he, your king, has all puissance.
In the name of the law, I command you, peace!
And King Herod—the devil run away with you!

HEROD:
Qui status in Jude et Rex Israel,
And the mightiest conqueror that ever walked on ground;
For I am even he that made both heaven and hell
And of my mighty power holdeth up this world round.
Magog and Madroke, both them I did confound,
And with this bright brand their bones I brake in sunder,
That all the wide world on those rappis did wonder.

I am the cause of this great light and thunder:
It is through my fury that they such noise do make.
My fearful countenance the clouds doth so encumber
That oft-times for dread thereof the very earth doth quake.
Look, when I with malice this bright brand doth shake,
All the whole world from the north to the south
I may them destroy with one word of my mouth.

To recount unto you my innumerable substance,
That were too much for any tongue to tell,
For all the whole orient is under my obedience,
And prince am I of purgatory and chief captain of hell;
And those tyrannous traitors by force I may compel
Mine enemies to vanquish and even to dust them drive,
That with a twinkle of mine eye not one to be left alive.

Behold my countenance and my colour,
Brighter than the sun in the middle of the day.
Where can you have a more greater succour
Than to behold my person that is so gay,
My falchion and my fashion, with my gorgeous array?
He that had the grace always thereon to think,
Live he might always without other meat or drink.

And this my triumphant fame most highly doth abound
Throughout this world in all regions abroad,
Resembling the favour of that most mighty Mahound,
From Jupiter by descent and cousin to the great god.
And named the most renownèd King Herod:
Which that all princes hath under subjection,
And all their whole power under my protection.

And therefore, my herald here called Calchas,
Warn thou every port, that no ships arrive
Nor also alien stranger through my realm pass
But they for their tribute do pay marks five.

Now speed thee forth hastily
For they that will the contrary
Upon a gallows hanged shall be
And by Mahound, of me they get no grace.

HERALD:
Now, Lord and master, in all the haste
Thy worthy will it shall be wrought,
And thy royal countries shall be passed
In as short a time as can be thought. (*Exit.*)

HEROD:

Now shall our regions throughout be sought
In every place both east and west;
If any caitiffs to me be brought
It shall be nothing for their best.
And the while that I do rest,
Trumpets, viols and other harmony
Shall bless the waking of my majesty. (*Exit.*)

BALTHASAR:

Now blessed be God of his tiding,
For yonder a bright star do I see:
Now the Saviour is with us abiding
As the prophets said that it should be.
They said there should a babe be born,
Coming of the root of Jesse,
To save mankind that was forlorn;
And truly come now is he.

Reverence and worship to him would I do,
As God and man, that all made of nought.
All the prophets accorded and said even so,
That with his precious blood mankind should be bought.
He grant me grace by yonder star that I see,
And into that place bring me,
That I may worship him with humility
And see his glorious face.

MELCHIOR:

Out of my way I deem that I am,
For tokens of this country can I none see.
Now, God that on earth madest man,
Send me some knowledge where that I be!
Yonder methinks a fair, bright star I see,
The which betokeneth the birth of a child
That hither is come to make man free,
He born of a maid and she nothing defiled.

To worship that child is mine intent,
Forth now will I take my way.
I trust some company God hath me sent,
For yonder I see a King labour on the way.
Towards him now will I ride.
Hark, comely king, I you pray,
Into what coast will ye this tide,
Or whither lies your journey?

JASPAR:
To seek a child is mine intent,
Of whom the prophets have meant.
The time is come now is he sent,
By yonder star here may you see.

MELCHIOR:
Sir, I pray you with your licence,
To ride with you into his presence;
To him will I offer frankincense,
For the head of the whole church shall he be.

BALTHASAR:
I ride wandering in ways wide
Over mountains and dales: I wot not where I am.
Now King of all Kings, send me such guide
That I might have knowledge of this country's name.
Ah! yonder I see a sight beseeming all afar,
The which betokens some news, as I trow,
As methinks a child appearing in a star;
I trust he be come that shall defend us from woe.

Two kings yonder I see and to them will I ride,
For to have their company—I trust they will me abide.
Hail, comely kings and gentle.
Good sirs, I pray ye, whither are ye bent?

JASPAR:
To seek a child is our intent,
Which betokens yonder star as you may see.

MELCHIOR:
To him I purpose this present.

BALTHASAR:
Sirs, I pray you and that right humbly,
With you that I may ride in company.

ALL:
To almighty God now pray we
That his precious person we may see. (*Exeunt.*)

HERALD:
Hail, lord most of might,
Thy commandment is right,
Into thy land is come this night
Three kings, and with them a great company.

HEROD:
What make these kings in this country?

HERALD:
To seek a king and a child, they say.

HEROD:
Of what age should he be?

HERALD:
Scarce twelve days old fully.

HEROD:
And was he so late born?

HERALD:
Yes, sir, so they showed me, this same day in the morn.

HEROD:
Now on pain of death bring them me beforn.
And therefore, Herald, hie thee now in haste,

In all speed that thou wert dight,
Or that those kings the country be past,
Look then bring them all three before my sight.
And in Jerusalem enquire more of that child.
But I warn thee that thy words be mild,
For that take thou heed, and craft thereto,
His power to foredo,
That those three kings may be beguiled.

HERALD:

Lord, I am ready at your bidding,
To serve thee as my lord and king.
For joy thereof, lo how I spring
With light heart and fresh gambolling
  Aloft here on this mould.

HEROD:

Then speed thee forth hastily,
And look that thou bear thee evenly.
And also I pray thee heartily
That thou do commend me
  Both to young and old.

    The HERALD *meets the* KINGS *coming in.*

HERALD:

Hail, sir kings, in your degree!
Herod, king of these countries wide
Desireth to speak with you all three
And for your coming he doth abide.

JASPAR:

Sir, at his will we be right ready.
Hie us brethren, to that lord's place.
To speak with him we shall be happy;
To see the child we seek may he grant us grace.

HERALD: (*to* HEROD)
Hail, lord without peer!
These three kings here have I brought.

HEROD:

Now welcome, sir kings, all together.
But of my bright mien, sirs, dread ye nought.
Sir kings, as I understand,
A star hath guided you into my land.
Wherein great care ye have found
By reason of her beams bright.
And now I pray you heartily
The truth that ye would certify,
How long is it surely
Since of that star you first had sight?

JASPAR:

Sir king, the very truth we say,
    And to set your mind at rest,
This same is even the twelfth day
    Since it appeared to us to be West.

HEROD:

Brothers, then is there no more to say,
But with heart and will keep ye your journey,
And come home by me this same way,
    Of your news that I may know.
Ye shall triumph in this country
And with great concord banquet with me
And that child myself then will I see
    And honour him also.

MELCHIOR:

Sir, your commandment will we fulfil
And humbly submit ourselves theretill.
He that wieldeth all things at will
The ready way us teach,
    Sir king, that we may pass your land in peace.

HEROD:

Yes, and walk softly even at your own ease.
Your passport for a hundred days

Here shall you have of clear command,
Our realm to travel any ways
Here shall you have by special grant.

BALTHASAR:

Now farewell, king of high degree,
Humbly of you our leave we take.

HEROD:

Then adieu, sir kings all three,
And while I live, be bold of me,
There is nothing in this country
   But for your own ye shall it take.

    The KINGS *retreat.*

Now these three kings are gone on their way.
Unwisely and unwittily have they all wrought.
When they come again, they shall die that same day,
And thus these vile wretches to death shall be brought.
   Such is my liking.
He that against my laws will hold,
Be he king or kaiser never so bold,
I shall him cast into cares cold
   And to death I shall them bring.

    HEROD *goes off: The* KINGS *reappear.*

JASPAR:

Oh blessed God, much is thy might!
   Where is the star that gave us light?

MELCHIOR:

Now kneel we down here in this presence,
Beseeching that Lord of high magnificence
That we may see his high excellence
   If that his sweet will be.

BALTHASAR:

Yonder, brother, I see the star,

Whereby I know he is not far.
Therefore, lords, go we near
  Into this poor place.

> *They go near to* JOSEPH *and* MARY *seated with the*
> CHILD *on her knee.*

JASPAR: (*kneeling*)
Hail, Lord that all this world hath wrought!
Hail, God and man in one together,
For thou hast made all things of nought,
Albeit that thou liest poorly here.
A cup full of gold I have thee brought
  In token that thou art without peer.

MELCHIOR:
Hail be thou, Lord of high magnificence!
  In token of priesthood and dignity of office,
To thee I offer a cup full of incense,
  For it behoveth thee to have such sacrifice.

BALTHASAR:
Hail be thou, Lord long looked for,
  I have brought thee myrrh for mortality
In token that thou shalt mankind restore
  To life by thy death upon a tree.

MARY:
God have mercy, kings on your goodness!
  By the guiding of the Godhead hither are ye sent.
The provision of my sweet Son your ways home bless,
  And ghostly reward you for your present.

> *The* KINGS *make obeisance.*

JASPAR:
Sir kings, after our promise,
Home by Herod I must needs go.

MELCHIOR:

Now truly, brother we can no less:
But I am so far weary I know not what to do.

BALTHASAR:

Right so am I: wherefore I you pray,
Let us all rest us awhile upon this ground.

MELCHIOR:

Brother, I am well pleased to do as you say.
The grace of that sweet child save us all sound! (*They sleep.*)

ANGEL:

King of Taurus, sir Jaspar,
King of Araby, sir Balthasar,
Melchior, King of Aginar,
To you now am I sent.
For dread of Herod, go you west home:
Into those parts when ye come down,
Ye shall be hailed with great renown.
The Holy Ghost this knowledge hath sent.

JASPAR:

Awake, sir kings, I you pray,
For the voice of an angel I heard in my dream.

MELCHIOR:

That is full true that ye do say,
For he rehearsed our names plain.

BALTHASAR:

He bade that we should go down by west,
For dread of Herod's false betray.

JASPAR:

So for to do it is the best.
The child that we have sought guide us the way!

Now farewell the fairest of shape so sweet!
And thanked be Jesus for his call,
That we three together so suddenly should meet,
That dwell so wide and in strange land,
And here make our presentation
Unto this King's son cleansed and so clean,
And to his mother, for our salvation;
Of much mirth now may we mean
That we so well have done this oblation.

MELCHIOR:

Now farewell, sir Jaspar, brother, to you
King of Taurus the most worth;
Sir Balthasar, also to you I bow;
And I thank you both of your good company
That we together have had.
He that made us to meet on hill,
I thank him now and ever I will;
For now may we go without ill
And of our offerings be full glad.

BALTHASAR:

Now sith that we must needly go
For dread of Herod that is so wroth,
Now farewell, brother, and brother also,
I take my leave of you both
This day on feet.
Now he that made us to meet on plain,
And offer to Mary and to her Son,
He give us grace in heaven again
All together to meet.

The KINGS *go.*

HERALD:

Hail, king most worthiest in weed!
Hail, maintainer of courtesy through all this world wide!
Hail, the most mightiest that ever bestrode a steed!

Hail, most manfullest man in armour man to abide!
Hail in thine honour!
These three kings that forth were sent
And should have come again before thee here present,
Another way, lord, home they went
Contrary to thine honour.

HEROD:

Another way? Out! Out! Out!
Hath those false traitors done me this deed?
I stamp! I stare! I look all about!
Might I them take I should them burn at a glede.
I rend! I roar! And now run I wood! *
Ah, that these villain traitors hath marred thus my mood!
They shall be hanged if I come them to.

> HEROD *rages in the pageant and in the street also.*

Eh, and that child of Bethlehem he shall be dead
And thus shall I foredo his prophecy.

How say you, sir Knights? Is not this the best rede
That all young children for this should be dead,
With sword to be slain?
Then shall I, Herod, live in fame
And all folk me doubt and dread
And offer me gold and riches for the same:
    Thereto will they be full fain.

FIRST SOLDIER:

My lord, King Herod by name,
    Thy words against my will shall be;
To see so many young childer die is shame,
    Therefore counsel thereto gettest thou none of me.

SECOND SOLDIER:

Well said, fellow, my troth I plight.
    Sir King, perceive right well you may,
So great a murder to see of young fruit
    Will make a rising in thine own country.

* Mad.

HEROD:

A rising? Out! Out! Out! (HEROD *rages again.*)
  Out! Villain wretches, harrow upon you I cry!
My will utterly look that it be wrought
  Or upon a gallows both you shall die,
By Mahound most mightiest that me dear hath bought.

FIRST SOLDIER:

Now, cruel Herod, since we shall do this deed—
  Your will needfully in this realm must be wrought—
All the children of that age die they must need;
  Now with all my might that shall be upsought.

SECOND SOLDIER:

And I will swear here upon your bright sword,
  All the childer that I find, slain they shall be;
That makes many a mother to weep and be full sore
    afeared,
  In our armour bright when they us see.

HEROD:

Now that ye have sworn, forth that ye go,
  And my will that ye work both by day and night,
And then will I for fain trip like a doe.
  But when they be dead, I warn you bring them before
    my sight.

  HEROD *and his train go away;* MARY *and* JOSEPH
  asleep, an angel comes.

ANGEL:

Mary and Joseph, to you I say,
  Sweet word from the Father I bring you full right:
Out of Bethlehem into Egypt forth go ye the way
  And with you take the King full of might,
    For dread of Herod's rede.

JOSEPH:

Arise up, Mary, hastily and soon;
Our Lord's will needs must be done,
Like as the angel us bade.

MARY:

Meekly, Joseph mine own spouse,
Towards that country let us repair;
In Egypt, to some token of house,
God grant us grace safe to come there.

*MARY and JOSEPH go clean away: the women come in
with their children, singing to them.*

WOMEN: (*sing*)

Lulla, lulla, thou little tiny child
By by, lully lullay thou little tiny child
By by lully lullay!

O sisters too
How may we do
For to preserve this day
This poor youngling
For whom we do sing
By by lully lullay!

Herod the king,
In his raging,
Charged he hath this day
His men of might
In his own sight
All young children to slay—

That woe is me
Poor child, for thee,
And ever morn and day
For thy parting
Neither say nor sing
By by lully lullay.

FIRST WOMAN:

I lull my child wondrously sweet
  And in mine arms I do it keep
    Because that it should not cry.

SECOND WOMAN:

That babe that is born in Bethlehem, so meek,
  He save my child and me from villainy!

THIRD WOMAN:

Be still, be still, my little child!
  That lord of lords he save both thee and me
For Herod hath sworn with words wild
  That all young children slain they shall be.

FIRST SOLDIER:

Say ye, widowed wives, whither are ye away?
  What bear you in your arms needs must we see.
If they be man-children, die they must this day,
  For at Herod's will all things must be.

SECOND SOLDIER:

When I them seize once into my hands
  Them for to slay will I not spare;
We must fulfil Herod's commands
  Else we be as traitors and cast all in care.

FIRST WOMAN:

Sir knights, of your courtesy,
  This day shame not your chivalry
But on my child have pity
  For my sake in this stead;
For a simple slaughter it would show
To work such a child woe
That can neither speak nor go
  Nor never harm did.

SECOND WOMAN:

He that slays my child in sight,

If that my stroke on him may light,
Be he squire or knight
   I hold him but lost.
So, thou false deceiver
A stroke shalt thou bear me here
   And spare for no cost.

THIRD WOMAN:

Sit he never so high in saddle,
But I shall make his brains addle,
And here with my pot-ladle
   With him will I fight.
I shall lay on him as though I wood were
With this same womanly gear;
There shall no man stir
   Whether that he be king or knight.

    The SOLDIERS *kill the children.*

FIRST SOLDIER:

Who heard ever such a cry
Of women that their children have lost
And greatly rebuking chivalry
   Throughout this realm in every coast
   Which many a man's life is like to cost?
     For this great wreak that here is done
     I fear much vengeance thereof will come.

SECOND SOLDIER:

Eh, brother, such tales may we not tell;
   Wherefore to the king let us go
For he is like to bear the peril
   Which was the causer that we did so.
   Yet must they all be brought him to
     With wains and waggons fully freight:
     I trow there will be a care-full sight.

FIRST SOLDIER:

Lo, Herod king, here must thou see
   How many thousand that we have slain.

SECOND SOLDIER:

And needs thy will fulfilled must be;
　There may no man say thereagain.

MESSENGER:

Herod king, I shall thee tell,
　All thy deeds is come to nought;
This child is gone into Egypt to dwell.
　Lo sir, in thine own land what wonders are wrought!

HEROD:

Into Egypt? Alas for woe!
　Longer in land I cannot abide;
Saddle my palfrey, for in haste will I go
　After yonder traitors now will I ride,
　　Them for to slay.
　　　Now all men hie fast
　　　Into Egypt in haste!
　　　All that country will I taste
　　Till I may them find and flay.

12

THE TEMPTATION OF CHRIST

York Locksmiths' Play

DEVIL:

> Make room! Be alive! And let me gang.
> What makes here all this madding throng?
> Hie you all hence! High might you hang,
> > Right with a rope.
> I dread me that I dwell too long
> > To do a jape.
> For since the first time that I fell
> For my high pride from heaven to hell,
> Ever have I mustered me to tell
> > Among mankind
> How I in dole might make them dwell,
> > There to be pined.
> And sure, all that have since been born
> Have come to me, mid-day and morn;
> I have ordained so therefor;
> > None may them fend,
> That from all liking they are lorn
> > Without an end.
> And now some men speak of a swain,
> How he shall come and suffer pain,
> And with his death to bliss again
> > They should be bought.
> But sure, this tale's but a trick and vain;
> > I trust it nought.
> For I know every deal, I ween,

Of this same minion that men mean,
How he has in great trouble been
    Since he was born,
And suffered mickle plots and pain,
    Both even and morn.
And now it is brought so about,
That lurdan that they love and lout,
To wilderness he is gone out,
    He and no mo.
To hurt him now I have no doubt,
    Betwixt us two.
Before this time he has been intent,
That I might get him with no glint;
But now since he so alone went,
    I shall essay,
And make him to some sin assent,
    If that I may.
He has fasted—that mars his mood—
These forty days now without food.
If he be man in bone and blood
    He hungers ill.
In gluttony then hold I good
    To wit his will.
For so it shall be known indeed
If the Godhead in him be hid.
If he will do as I him bid,
    When I come near—
There was never deed that ever he did
    To grieve him more.
Thou witty man and wise of rede,
If thou can ought of Godhead,
Bid now that these stones be made bread
    Betwixt us two.
Then may they stand thyself in stead
    And others too.
For thou hast fasted long, I ween;
I would now that some meat were seen,

For old acquaintance us between;
  Thyself knows how.
There shall no man know what I mean,
  But I and thou.

JESUS:

  My Father, that all sorrow may slake,
Honour evermore I to thee make,
And gladly suffer for thy sake
   Such villainy.
And thus temptation for to take
   Of mine enemy.
Thou wicked wight, thy wits are gone.
For written it is, whoso has understood,
A man lives not in main and mood
   With bread alone,
But God's own words are ghostly food
   To men each one.
If I have fasted, 'tis of skill.
Wit thou, I hunger not so ill
That I work not my Father's will
   In all degree.
Thy bidding will I not fulfil;
   That I warn thee.

DEVIL:

  Away! Such talking never I kenned.
He hungers not so as I weened.
Now since thy Father may thee fend
   By subtle sleight,
Let see if thou alone may land
   There upon height,
Upon the pinnacle perfectly—
Aha! Now go we well thereby.
I shall essay in vainglory
   To make him fall.
And if he be God's Son mighty,
   Surely I shall.
Now list to me a little space.

If thou be God's Son full of grace,
Show some affair here in this place,
  To prove thy might.
Let's see . . . Fall down upon thy face,
  Here in my sight.
For it is written, as well is kenned,
How God shall angels to thee send,
And they shall keep thee in their hand
  Whereso thou goes,
That thou shall on no stone descend
  To hurt thy toes.
Since thou may with no danger, i'faith,
Fall so and do thyself no scathe,
Then tumble down to ease us both,
  Here to my feet.
If thou do not, I shall be wroth;
  That shalt thou see.

JESUS:

  Let be, warlock, thy words all vain.
  For written it is full clear and plain,
  "Thy God thou shalt not tempt with pain
    Nor with discord,
  Nor quarrel shalt thou none maintain
    Against thy Lord."
  And therefore trow thou yet again
  That all thy gauds shall nothing gain.
  Be subject to thy sovereign
    Early and late.

DEVIL:

  What! All this travail is in vain,
    By ought I wot.
  He proves that he is mickle of price;
  There it is good I me advise;
  And since I may not in this wise
    Make him my thrall,
  I shall essay in covetise
    To make him fall.

For sure, I shall not leave him yet.
Who is my sovereign, I would wit?
Myself ordained thee there to sit;
  This wot you well.
And right even as I ordained it
  Is done each deal.
Then mayest thou see, since it is so,
That I am sovereign of us two.
And yet I grant thee ere I go,
  And without fail,
That if thou wilt assent me to,
  It shall avail.
For I have all this world to wield,
Tower and town, forest and field;
If thou thine heart will to me yield
  With word full kind,
Yet will I surely be thy shield
  And faithful friend.
Behold now, sir, and you shall see
Many a kingdom, many a country;
All this here will I give to thee
  For evermore,
If thou wilt fall and honour me,
  As I said ere.

JESUS:

Cease of thy saws, thou Sathanas.
I grant no thing that you me ask.
To pine of hell I bid thee pass
  And swiftly wend,
And dwell in woe, as thou ere was,
  Without an end.
No other might shall be thy meed.
For written it is, who right can read,
The Lord thy God thou ought to dread
  And honour aye,
And serve him in thy word and deed,
  Both night and day.
And since thou does not as I thee tell,

No longer will I let thee dwell.
I command thee, thou hie to hell,
    And hold thee there,
With fellowship of fiends fell
    For evermore.

DEVIL:

Out! I dare not look, alas!
It is worse than ever it was.
He musters all the might he has.
    High might he hang!
It follows fast, for I must pass
    To torments strong.

FIRST ANGEL:

Ah, mercy, Lord. What may this mean?
I marvel that you bear this pain
Of this foul fiend artful and keen
    Talking to you.
And you his wickedness, I ween,
    May waste at will.
Methinks that you were straitly stead,
Lord, with this fiend that now is fled.

JESUS:

Mine angel dear, be not adread;
    He may not grieve.
The Holy Ghost aye has me led;
    Thus now believe.
For when the fiend shall my folk see
Assailing them in sore degree,
Their mirror may they make of me,
    For to stand still.
For overcome they shall not be,
    But if they will.

SECOND ANGEL:

Ah, Lord, this is a great meekness
In you in whom all mercy is,

And at your will may doom or dress,
        As is worthy;
And three temptations takes express
        Thus sovereignly.

JESUS:

My blessing have they with my hand
That with such grief grudge not nor bend,
And also that will stiffly stand
        Against the fiend.
I know my time is fast at hand.
        Now will I wend.

13

THE WOMAN TAKEN IN ADULTERY

Hegge Cycle

JESUS: (*speaks to the audience*)
    Nolo mortem pecatoris.
    Man, for thy sin take repentance;
    If thou amend that is amiss,
    Then heaven shall be thine inheritance.
    Though thou have done against God grievance,
    Yet mercy to ask look thou be bold;
    His mercy does pass, in true balance,
    All cruel judgment by manifold.

    Though that your sins be never so great,
    For them be sad and ask mercy;
    Soon of my Father grace ye may get,
    With the least tear weeping out of your eye.
    My Father me sent thee, man, to buy:
    All thy ransom myself must pay,
    For love of thee myself will die;
    If thou ask mercy, I say never nay.

    Unto the earth from heaven above,
    Thy sorrow to cease and joy to restore,
    Man, I came down all for thy love;
    Love me again, I ask no more.
    Though thou mishap and sin the most,
    Yet turn again and mercy crave.
    It is thy fault if thou be lost;
    Ask thou mercy and thou shalt have.

Upon thy neighbour be not vengeful,
Against the law if he offend.
Like as he is, thou art unstable;
Thine own frailty ever thou attend.
Evermore thy neighbour help to amend,
Even as thou wouldest he should thee;
Against him wrath if thou accend,
The same in hap will fall on thee.

Each man to other be merciable,
And mercy he shall have at need;
What man of mercy is not capable,
When he asketh mercy he shall not speed.
Mercy to grant I come indeed;
Who ask mercy he shall have grace;
Let no man doubt for his misdeed,
But ever ask mercy while he hath space.

SCRIBE:

Alas, alas, our law is lorn!
A false hypocrite, Jesu by name,
That of a shepherd's daughter was born,
Will break our law and make it lame.
He will us work right mickle shame,
His false purpose if he uphold;
All our laws he doth defame—
That stinking beggar is wondrous bold!

PHARISEE:

Sir scribe, in faith that hypocrite
Will turn this land all to his lore;
Therefore I counsel him to indict,
And chastise him right well therefor.

SCRIBE:

On him believe many a score,
In his preaching he is so gay;
Each man him followeth more and more;
Against that he saith no man saith nay.

PHARISEE:

> A false quarrel if we could feign,
> That hypocrite to put in blame,
> His preaching men should soon disdain,
> And then his worship should turn to shame.
> With some falsehood to spill his name,
> Let us essay his lore to spill;
> The people 'gainst him if we could inflame
> Then should we soon have all our will.

ACCUSER:

> Hark, sir pharisee, and sir scribe!
> A right good sport I can you tell;
> I undertake that right a good bribe
> We all shall have to keep counsel.
> A fair young quean hereby doth dwell,
> Both fresh and gay upon to look,
> And a tall man with her doth mell:
> The way unto her chamber right even he took.

> Let us three now go straight thither;
> The way full even I shall you lead;
> And we shall take them both together,
> While that they do that sinful deed.

SCRIBE:

> Art thou certain that we shall speed?
> Shall we him find when we come there?

ACCUSER:

> By my troth, I have no dread
> The hare from the form we shall arear.

PHARISEE:

> We shall have game if this be true.
> Let us three work by one assent:
> We will her bring even before Jesu,
> And of her life the truth present,

How in adultery her life is lent.
Then him before when she is brought,
We shall him ask the true judgment,
What lawful death to her is wrought.
Of grace and mercy ever he doth preach,
And that no man should be vengeful.
Against the woman if he say wreak,
Then of his preaching he is unstable;
And if we find him variable
Of his preaching that he hath taught,
Then have we cause, both just and able,
For a false man that he be caught.

SCRIBE:

Now, by great God, ye say full well!
If we find him in variance,
We have good reason, as ye do tell,
Him for to bring to foul mischance.
If he hold still his dalliance,
And preach of mercy, her for to save,
Then have we matter of great substance
Him for to kill and put in grave.

Great reason why I shall you tell:
For Moses in our law doth ordain
That every adulterer we should quell,
And that with stones they should be slain.
Against Moses' law if that he slip,
That sinful woman with grace to help,
He shall never escape out of our grip,
But he shall die like a dog whelp.

ACCUSER:

Ye tarry over-long, sirs, I say you;
They will soon part, as that I guess;
Therefore if ye will have your prey now,
Let us go take them in their wantonness.

PHARISEE:

> Go thou before, the way to dress;
> We shall thee follow within short while.
> If that we may that quean distress,
> I hope we shall Jesu beguile.

SCRIBE:

> Break up the door and go we in;
> Set to the shoulder with all thy might.
> We shall take them even in their sin;
> Their own trespass shall them indict.

> > *Here a young man runs out in his doublet, with shoes untied and holding up his breeches with his hand.*

ACCUSER:

> Stop that harlot, some earthly wight,
> That in adultery here is found.

YOUNG MAN:

> If any man stop me this night,
> I shall give him a deadly wound.

> If any man my way doth stop,
> Ere we depart dead shall he be:
> I shall this dagger put in his crop;
> I shall him kill ere he shall me.

PHARISEE:

> May Great God's curse go with thee!
> With such a shrew will I not mell.

YOUNG MAN:

> That same blessing I give you three,
> And bequeath you all to the devil of hell.
> > *To audience.*
> In faith, I was so sore afraid
> Of yon three shrews, the sooth to say,

My breech be not yet well uptied;
I had such haste to run away.
They shall never catch me in such a fray;
I am full glad that I am gone.
Adieu, adieu, in twenty devils' way!
And God's curse have ye every one.

SCRIBE:

Come forth, thou stot; come forth, thou scout!
Come forth, thou bismer and brothel bold!
Come forth, thou whore and stinking bitch-clout!
How long has thou such harlotry hold?

PHARISEE:

Come forth, thou quean; come forth, thou scold!
Come forth, thou sloven; come forth, thou slut!
We shall thee teach with cares cold
A little better to keep thy cut.

WOMAN:

Ah, mercy, mercy, sirs, I you pray;
For God's love have mercy on me!
Of my misliving me not bewray:
Have mercy on me, for charity!

ACCUSER:

Ask us no mercy; it shall not be.
We shall so ordain for thy lot
That thou shalt die for thine adultery;
Therefore come forth, thou stinking stot!

WOMAN:

Sirs, my honour if ye will save,
And help I have no open shame,
Both gold and silver ye shall have,
So that in cleanness ye keep my name.

SCRIBE:

Meed for to take, we were to blame,
To save such stots; it shall not be.

We shall bring thee to such a game
That all adulterers shall learn by thee.

WOMAN:

Since that ye will not grant me grace,
But for my sin that I shall die,
I pray you kill me here in this place,
And let not the people upon me cry.
If I be slandered openly,
To all my friends it shall be shame;
I pray you kill me privily;
Let not the people know my defame.

PHARISEE:

Fie on thee, scout! The devil thee quell!
Against the law shall we thee kill?
First shall hang thee the devil of hell,
Ere we such follies should fulfil.
Though it like thee never so ill,
Before the prophet thou shalt be ta'en
Like as Moses doth charge us till,
With great stones thou shalt be slain.

ACCUSER:

Come forth apace, thou stinking scout!
Before the prophet thou shalt be ta'en.
Like as Moses doth charge us till,
With great stones thou shalt be slain.

SCRIBE:

Now, by great God, if I thee pay,
Such a buffet I shall thee take
That all the teeth, I dare well say,
Within thy head for it shall shake.

They take her to JESUS.

PHARISEE:

Hark, sir prophet! We all you pray

To give true doom and just sentence
Upon this woman, which this same day
In sinful adultery hath done offence.

> *Here* JESUS, *while they are accusing the woman,*
> *shall all the time write on the ground with his*
> *finger.*

ACCUSER:

See, we have brought her to your presence
Because ye be a wise prophet,
That ye shall tell by conscience
What death to her ye think most meet.

SCRIBE:

In Moses' law right thus we find:
That such false lovers shall be slain;
Straight to a stake we shall them bind,
And with great stones burst out their brain.
Of your conscience tell us the plain,
With this woman what shall be wrought:
Shall we let her go free again,
Or to her death shall she be brought?

> JESUS *does not reply, but goes on writing on the*
> *ground.*

WOMAN:

Now, holy prophet, be merciable!
Upon me, wretch, take no vengeance.
For my sins abominable,
In heart I have great repentance.
I am well worthy to have mischance,
Both bodily death and worldly shame;
But, gracious prophet, of succurrance
This time I pray you, for God's name.

PHARISEE:

Against the law thou didst offence,
Therefore of grace speak thou no more;

As Moses gives in law sentence,
Thou shalt be stoned to death therefor.

ACCUSER:

Have done, sir prophet, tell us your lore:
Shall we this woman with stones kill,
Or to her house, her home, restore?
In this matter tell us your will.

SCRIBE:

In a cold study methinketh ye sit;
Good sir, awake, tell us your thought:
Shall she be stoned?—tell us your wit—
Or in what rule shall she be brought?

JESUS:

Look which of you that never sin wrought,
But is of life cleaner than she;
Cast at her stones, and spare her nought,
Clean out of sin if that ye be.

> *Here* JESUS, *again stooping down, shall write on
> the ground, and all the accusers, as if put to
> shame, shall go apart into three separate places.*

PHARISEE:

Alas, alas, I am ashamed!
I am afeard that I shall die;
All my sins, even properly named,
Yon prophet did write before mine eye.
If that my fellows that did espy,
They will tell it both far and wide;
My sinful living if they out cry,
I wot never where my head to hide.

ACCUSER:

Alas, for sorrow mine heart doth bleed!
All my sins yon man did write;
If that my fellows to them took heed,
I cannot me from death acquit.

I would I were hid somewhere out of sight,
That men should me nowhere see nor know;
If I be take, I am affright
In mickle shame I shall be thrown.

SCRIBE:

Alas the time that this betid!
Right bitter care doth me embrace;
All my sins be now unhid:
Yon man before me them all doth trace.
If I were once out of this place,
To suffer death great and vengeance able,
I will never come before his face,
Though I should die in a stable.

WOMAN:

Though I be worthy for my trespass
To suffer death abominable,
Yet, holy prophet, of your high grace,
In your judgment be merciable.
I will never more be so unstable:
O holy prophet, grant me mercy!
For my sins unreasonable
With all my heart I am sorry.

JESUS:

Where be thy foemen that did thee accuse?
Why have they left us two alone?

WOMAN:

Because they could not themselves excuse,
With shame they fled hence every one.
But, gracious prophet, list to my moan:
Of my sorrow take compassion;
Now all my enemies hence be gone,
Say me some word of consolation.

JESUS:

For those sins that thou hast wrought
Hath any man condemned thee?

WOMAN:

> Nay, forsooth, that hath there nought;
> But in your grace I put me.

JESUS:

> For me thou shalt not condemned be;
> Go home again and walk at large:
> Look that thou live in honesty,
> And will no more to sin, I thee charge.

WOMAN:

> I thank you highly, holy prophet,
> Of this great grace ye have me grant;
> All my lewd life I shall down let,
> And try to be God's true servant.

JESUS:

> What man of sin be repentant,
> Of God if he will mercy crave,
> God of mercy is so abundant,
> That what man ask it he shall it have.

> *To the audience.*

> When man is contrite and hath won grace,
> God will not keep old wrath in mind;
> But better love to them he has,
> Very contrite when he them find.
> Now God, that died for all mankind,
> Save all these people both night and day;
> And of our sins he us unbind,
> High Lord of heaven that best may.   **Amen.**

14

PALM SUNDAY

York Skinners' Play

JESUS:
> To me take tent and give good heed,
> My dear disciples that be here.
> I shall tell you that shall be indeed.
> My time to pass hence draweth near,
>> And by this skill,
> Man's soul to save from sorrows sore,
>> That lost was ill.
> From heaven to earth when I descend,
> Ransom to make I made promise.
> The prophecy now draws to an end;
> My father's will forsooth it is
>> That sent me hither.
> Peter, Philip, I shall you bless,
>> And go together
> Unto yon castle that is you again.
> Go with good heart and tarry not.
> My commandment to do be ye fain;
> As I charge you, look it be wrought.
>> There shall ye find
> An ass, there fast as you had sought;
>> Then her unbind
> With her foal, and to me them bring,
> That I on her may sit a space;
> So the prophecy clear meaning
> May be fulfilled here in this place:
>> "Daughter of Sion,

Lo, thy lord comes riding on an ass,
    Thee to open."
If any man will you gainsay,
Say that your lord has need of them,
And shall restore them this same day
Unto what man will then them claim.
    Do thus this thing.
Go forth ye both, and aye remain
    In my blessing.

PETER:

    Jesu, Master, even at thy will
    And at thy list we like to do.
    Yon beast which thou desirest still
    Even at thy will shall come thee to,
        Unto thine ease.
    Surely, Lord, we will thither, all
        Thee for to please.

PHILIP:

    Lord, thee to please we are full fain,
    Both night and day to do thy will.
    Go we, brother, with all our main,
    My Lord's desire for to fulfil.
        For prophecy,
    We must it do to him by skill
        To do duly.

PETER:

    Yea, brother Philip. Behold, surely!
    For as he said we soon should find,
    Methinks yon beasts before mine eye,
    They are the same we should unbind.
        Therefore freely
    Go we to him that did them bind,
        And ask meekly.

PHILIP:

    The beasts are common, well I know,
    Therefore we need to ask less leave,

And our Master shall keep the law.
We may take them straight, I believe,
    For nought we let.
Full well I wit our time is brief;
    Go we them get.

PORTER:

Say,
What are ye makes here mastery,
To loose these beasts sans livery?
You seem too bold, for nothing ye
Have here to do; therefore rede I
    Such things to cease,
Or else ye may fall in folly
    And great disease.

PETER:

Sir, with your leave heartily we pray
This beast that we might have.

PORTER:

To what intent, first shall ye say,
And then I grant what you will crave
    By good reason.

PHILIP:

Our master, sir, that all may save
    Asks for this one.

PORTER:

What a man is't that ye master call?
Such privilege how dare he claim?

PETER:

Jesus, who of Jews is king and ever shall,
Prophet of Nazareth by name,
    This same is he;
Both God and man without all blame,
    That trust well we.

PORTER:

> Sirs, of that prophet heard I have;
> But tell me first plain, where is he?

PHILIP:

> He comes at hand, so God me save;
> That Lord we left at Bethphage,
> > He bides us there.

PORTER:

> Sir, take this beast, with heart full free,
> > And forth now fare.
> And if thou think it should be done,
> I shall declare plain his coming
> To the chief of the Jews, that they may soon
> Assemble them to his meeting.
> > What is your rede?

PETER:

> Thou sayest full well in thy meaning;
> > Do forth thy deed.
> And soon this beast we shall thee bring,
> And it restore, as reason will.

PORTER:

> These tidings shall have no hiding,
> But to the citizens declare I still
> > Of this city;
> I suppose freely that they will
> > Meet him with me.
> And since I will they warned be,
> Both young and old, of every state,
> For his coming I will them meet,
> To let them know, without debate—
> > Lo, where they stand,
> These citizens chief in their estate
> > Of all this land.
> He that is ruler of all right

And freely shaped both sand and sea
Save you now, lordlings gaily dight,
And keep you in your seemlity,
     And all honour.

FIRST BURGESS:

Welcome, Porter. What novelty,
     Tell us, this hour?

PORTER:

Sir, novelty I can you tell,
And trust that fully as for true.
Here comes of kin of Israel
At hand the prophet called Jesu,
     Lo, this same day,
Riding on an ass; this tidings true
     Conceive ye may.

SECOND BURGESS:

And is that prophet Jesus near?
Of him I have heard great marvels told.
He does great wonders, as I hear;
He heals the sick, both young and old;
     The blind—gives them their sight;
Both dumb and deaf, as himself would,
     He cures them right.

THIRD BURGESS:

Yea,
Five thousand men with loaves but five
He fed, and each one had enow;
Water to wine he turned rife;
He made corn grow without a plough,
     Where ere was none.
To dead men also he gave life—
     Lazar was one.

FOURTH BURGESS:

> Oft in our Temple has he preached
> Against the people that lived wrong,
> And also new laws has he teached
> Against our laws we used so long,
>> And said plainly,
> The old shall waste, the new shall gang—
>> That we shall see.

FIFTH BURGESS:

> Yea, Moyses' law he know each deal,
> And all the prophets in a row;
> He tells them so each man may feel
> And that they may entirely know,
>> If ought were dim;
> What prophets have said in their saw
>> Belongs to him.

SIXTH BURGESS:

> Emmanuel also by right
> They call that prophet, as cause will;
> He is the same that once was hight
> By Ysaye before, who still
>> Thus said full clear,
> "Lo, a maiden that knew never ill
>> A child should bear."

SEVENTH BURGESS:

> King David spoke of him, I ween,
> And left witness, ye know each one.
> He said the fruit of his flesh clean
> Should royal reign upon his throne,
>> And therefore he
> Of David's kin and other none
>> Our king shall be.

EIGHTH BURGESS:

> Methinks, good sirs, ye say right well,
> And good examples forth ye bring.
> And since we thus this matter feel,
> Go we, meet him as our own king,
>> And king him call.
> What is your counsel in this thing?
>> Now say ye all.

FIRST BURGESS:

> Against reason I will not plead,
> For well I wot our king he is.
> Whoso against his king will threat,
> He is not wise; he does amiss.
>> Porter, come near.
> What knowledge hast thou of his coming?
>> Tell us all here,
> And then we will go meet him free,
> And him honour, as well we owe,
>> Worthily to our city,
> And for our sovereign lord him know,
>> In whom we trust.

PORTER:

> Sir, I will tell you all on row,
>> If ye will list.
> Of his disciples two this day
> Where that I stood, they fair me greet,
> And on their lord's behalf did pray
> Our common ass that they might get
>> But for a while,
> Whereon their master soft might sit,
>> Space of a mile.
> And all this matter they me told
> Right wholly as I say to you,
> And the ass they have right as they would,
> And soon will bring again, I trow;
>> So they professed.

What ye will do, advise you now;
 Thus think I best.

SECOND BURGESS:

 Truly then as for me I say,
 I rede we make us ready anon;
 Him to greet goodly go this day,
 And him receive with great renown,
  As worthy is;
 And therefore, sirs, in field and town
  Fulfil ye this.

PORTER:

 Yea, and your children with you take,
 Though all in age they be full young;
 Ye may fare better for their sake,
 Through blessing of so good a king.
  This is no doubt.

THIRD BURGESS:

 I give thee thank for thy saying.
  We will him lout.
 And him to meet I am right fain,
 In the best manner that I can;
 For I desire to see him plain
 And honour him as his own man,
  Since sooth I see.
 King of Jews will we call him then;
  Our king is he.

FOURTH BURGESS:

 Our king is he; that is no lies.
 Our law to it accords full well.
 The prophets all bear full witness,
 Who of his secret truth could tell,
  And thus would say,
 "Amongst ourselves shall come great weal,
  Through God's own way."

FIFTH BURGESS:

> This same is he—there is none other—
> Was promised us full long before.
> For Moses said, who is our brother,
> A new prophet God should restore.
>> Therefore look ye
> What ye will do. Delay no more.
>> Our king is he.

SIXTH BURGESS:

> Of Juda comes our king so free,
> Of Jesse, David, Salamon.
> Also by his mother's kin, see ye,
> The genealogy bears witness on;
>> This is right plain.
> Him to honour right as I can
>> I am full fain.

SEVENTH BURGESS:

> Of this conceit of your clean wit
> I am full glad in heart and thought,
> And to meet him I will not let;
> I am ready, and will feign nought,
>> But with you come
> To him who bliss again has brought
>> With mirth and game.

EIGHTH BURGESS:

> Your arguments, they are so clear,
> I gainsay not, but grant you still.
> For when I of that counsel hear,
> I covet him with fervent will
>> Once for to see.
> I trow I from henceforward shall
>> Better man be.

FIRST BURGESS:

> Go we then with procession
> To meet him comely, as we owe,
> With branches, flowers and unison,
> And mighty songs here in a row.
> > Our children shall
> Go sing before, that men may know
> > This grant we all.

PETER:

> Jesu, my Lord and master free,
> As thy command, so have we done.
> This ass here we have brought to thee.
> What is thy will? Now show us soon,
> > And tarry not;
> And then we shall, delay to shun,
> > Fulfil thy thought.

JESUS:

> I thank you, brethren mild of mood.
> Do on this ass your clothes now lay,
> And lift me up with hearts right good,
> That I on her may sit this day
> > In my blessing.

PHILIP:

> Lord, thy will to do alway
> > We grant all things.

JESUS:

> And now, my brethren, with good cheer
> Give good intent, for ride I will
> Unto yon city ye see so near;
> Ye shall me follow together still,
> > As I ere said.

PHILIP:

>Lord, on our life, with all good will
>>We hold us glad.

BLIND MAN:

>Ah Lord, that all this world has made,
>Both sun and moon and night and day,
>What noise is this that makes me glad?
>From whence it comes I cannot say,
>>Or what it mean.
>If any man walk in this way,
>>Say what is seen.

POOR MAN:

>Why, man, what ails thee so to cry?
>Where would thou be? Now tell me here.

BLIND MAN:

>Ah, sir, a poor blind man am I,
>And aye have been from tender year,
>>Since I was born.
>I heard a voice of noble cheer,
>>Here me before.

POOR MAN:

>Man, wilt thou ought that I can do?

BLIND MAN:

>Yea, sir; for gladly would I wit,
>If thou would ought declare me to—
>This mirth I heard, what mean may it
>>To understand?

POOR MAN:

>Jesus the prophet full of grace
>>Comes here at hand,
>And all the citizens from town
>Go him to meet with melody,

With the fairest procession
That was ever seen in this Jewry.
   He is right near.

BLIND MAN:

 Sir, help me to the street hastily,
   That I may hear
 That noise, and that I might through grace—
 My sight of him to crave I would.

POOR MAN:

 Lo, he is here at this same place.
 Cry fast on him; look thou be bold,
   With voice right high.

BLIND MAN:

 Jesu, Thou Son of David called,
   Have thou mercy.
 Alas! I cry, he hears me not;
 He has no ruth for my misfare.
 He turns his ear. Where is his thought?

POOR MAN:

 Cry somewhat louder; do not spare.
   So may you speed.

BLIND MAN:

 Jesu, thou salver of all sore,
   To me give good heed.

PHILIP:

 Cease, man, and cry not so.
 The prince of the people goes thee by.
 Thou should sit still and attend thereto.
 Here passes the prophet of mercy;
   Thou dost amiss.

BLIND MAN:

> Ah, David's son, to thee I cry,
>> The king of bliss.

PETER:

> Lord, have mercy and let him go;
> He cannot cease of his crying.
> He follows us both to and fro;
> Grant him his boon and his asking,
>> And let him wend.
> We get no rest until this thing
>> Be brought to end.

JESUS:

> What wouldst thou, man, I to thee did?
> In this presence, tell openly.

BLIND MAN:

> Lord, mine eyesight from me is hid;
> Grant it to me, I cry mercy.
>> This would I have.

JESUS:

> Look up now with cheer blithely.
>> Thy faith can save.

BLIND MAN:

> Worship and honour aye to thee,
> With all service that can be done!
> The king of bliss, loved might he be,
> That thus my sight has sent me soon,
>> And by great skill.
> I was as blind as any stone;
>> I see at will.

LAME MAN:

> Ah, well were them that ever had life,
> Old or young, which ever it were,

Might wield their limbs free without strife,
Go with this mirth which I see here,
        And continue;
For I am set in sorrows sore
        That aye are new.
Thou Lord that shaped both night and day,
Of thy mercy have mind on me,
And help me, lord, as well you may.
        I may not gang;
For I am lame, as men may see,
        And have been long.
For well I know, as known is rife,
Both dumb and deaf, thou grantest them grace;
And to the dead thou hast given life.
Therefore grant me, Lord, in this place
        My limbs to wield.

JESUS:

Man, rise; cast thy crutches forth good space,
        Here in the field.
And look in truth thou steadfast be,
And follow me forth with good meaning.

LAME MAN:

Lord, lo, my crutches, where they flee
As far as I may let them fling
        With both my hands.
That ever again we have meeting,
        That now is banned.
For I was halt of limb and lame,
And I suffered pain and sorrows enow.
Everlasting Lord, loved by thy name.
I am as light as bird on bough.
        Aye be thou blest!
Such grace hast thou showed unto me,
    · Lord, as thou list.

ZACHEUS:

Since first this world was made of nought,
And all things set in equity,

Such wondrous thing was never wrought
As men this time may see with eye.
      What may it mean?
I cannot say what it may be,
      Comfort or pain.
And chiefly of a prophet new
That makes much profit, and of late
Both day and night to him they sue,
Our people all, through street and gate,
      New laws to hear.
Our old laws outworn now they hate,
      But hold his dear.
From death to life men will he raise,
To blind and dumb give speech and sight;
Greatly therefore our folk him praise,
And follow him both day and night
      From town to town.
They call him prophet by good right,
      As of renown.
And yet I marvel of that thing,
Since prince of publicans am I,
Of him I could have no knowing,
For all I would have come him nigh,
      Early and late.
Yet I am low, and of my height
      Full is the gate.
But since no better may befall,
I think what best is for to do.
I am so short, ye know well all,
Therefore yon tree I will go to,
      And in it climb.
Whether he come or pass me fro,
      I shall see him.
Ah, noble tree, thou sycamore,
I bless him that thee on earth brought.
Now may I see both here and there,
That under me it may be nought.
      Therefore in thee

Will I bide high in heart and thought,
    Till I him see.
Until the prophet come to town,
Here will I bide, whatso befall.

JESUS:

    Zacheus, do thou fast come down.

ZACHEUS:

    Lord, at thy will in haste I shall,
        And tarry not.
    To thee on knees, Lord, here I fall,
        For sin I wrought.
    And welcome, prophet trusty and true,
    With all those that to thee belong.

JESUS:

    Zachee, thy service new
    Shall make thee clear of all the wrong
        That thou has done.

ZACHEUS:

    Lord, I spare not for all this throng
        Here to say soon,
    My sin shames me, but not to repent.
    I sin forsake; therefore I will
    Have all my good that is unspent
    Unto poor folk to give them still;
        This will I fain.
    Whom I beguiled, to them I will
        Make right again.

JESUS:

    Thy clear confession shall thee cleanse;
    Thou mayest be sure of lasting life.
    Unto thy house, without offence,
    Is granted peace all without strife.
        Farewell, Zachee.

ZACHEUS:

> Lord, worship thee aye man and wife.
>> Blest might thou be.

JESUS:

> My dear disciples, behold and see.
> Unto Jerusalem we shall ascend.
> Man's son shall there betrayed be,
> And given into his enemies' hand
>> With great despite.
> Their spitting on him shall they spend,
>> And smartly smite.
> Peter, take thou this ass me fro,
> And lead it where thou first it took.
> I mourn, I sigh, I weep also,
> Jerusalem, on thee to look,
>> And so may you,
> That ever you your king forsook
>> And was untrue.
> For stone on stone shall none be left;
> Down to the ground shall all be cast;
> Thy game, thy glee, all from thee reft,
> And all for sin that thou done hast.
>> Thou art unkind.
> Against thy king thou hast trespassed.
>> Have this in mind.

PETER:

> Porter, take here thine ass again;
> At hand my lord comes on his feet.

PORTER:

> Behold, where all the burghers' train
> Come now with worship him to meet.
>> Therefore I will
> Let him abide here in this street,
>> And lout him still.

FIRST BURGESS:

Hail, prophet proved without a peer!
Hail, prince of peace shall ever endure!
Hail, king comely, courteous and clear!
Hail, sovereign seemly to sinful sore!
    To thee all bows.
Hail, lord lovely our cares to cure!
    Hail, King of Jews!

SECOND BURGESS:

Hail, flourishing flower that ne'er shall fade!
Hail, violet vernal with sweet odour!
Hail, mark of mirth, our medecine made!
Hail, blossom bright; hail, our succour;
    Hail, king comely!
Hail, worshipful! We thee honour
    With heart freely.

THIRD BURGESS:

Hail, David's son, doughty in deed!
Hail, rose ruddy; hail, beryl clear!
Hail, well of wealth that makes our meed!
Hail, salver of our sores severe!
    We worship thee.
Hail, gentle one with solace sure!
    Welcome thou be.

FOURTH BURGESS:

Hail, blissful babe in Bethleme born!
Hail, help of all our bitter bales!
Hail, lord that shaped both even and morn!
Hail, talker trustful of true tales!
    Hail, comely knight!
Hail, man of mood that most prevails
    To save aright!

FIFTH BURGESS:

Hail, diamond with jewels dight!
Hail, jasper gentle of Jewry!

Hail, lily lovesome, gleaming light!
Hail, balm of healing moist and dry
    To all in need!
Hail, bairn most blest of mild Mary!
    Hail, all our meed!

SIXTH BURGESS:

Hail, conqueror; hail, most of might!
Hail, ransomer of sinners all!
Hail, pitiful! Hail, lovely light!
Hail! Welcome of us shall on thee fall.
    Hail, royal Jew!
Hail, comely corse that we thee call,
    With mirth still new!

SEVENTH BURGESS:

Hail, sun aye shining with bright beams!
Hail, lamp of life that ne'er shall waste!
Hail, lucid lantern's lovely gleams!
Hail, text of truth so true to taste!
    Hail, king and sire!
Hail, maiden's child that graced her most!
    We thee desire.

EIGHTH BURGESS:

Hail, doomsman dread that all shall doom!
Hail, that all quick and dead shall lout!
Hail, whom worship shall most beseem!
Hail, whom all things shall dread and doubt!
    We welcome thee
Hail and welcome of all about,
    To our city!

15

THE SECOND TRIAL BEFORE PILATE:
THE SCOURGING AND CONDEMNATION

York Tilemakers' Play

PILATE:
Lordings, that are limited to the law of my alliance,
Ye shapely soldiers all shining to show,
I charge you as your chieftain that ye chat for no chance,
But look to your lord here and learn at my law.
As a duke I may condemn you and draw;
Many bold bairns are about me;
And what knight or knave I may know,
That lists not as a lord for to lout me,
  I shall learn him
In the devil's name, that dastard, to fear me.
Yea, who works any works without me,
I shall charge him in chains to cheer him.
Therefore, my lusty lads within this land lapped,
Stint now stepping softly and stoutly be bearing.
The traitor with tales who his tongue has trapped,
That fiend for his flattery full foul shall be falling.
What brat over broadly is brawling,
Or unsoftly will say in these halls,
That caitiff thus crying and calling,
As a boy shall be brought into bales.
  Therefore,
Talk not nor treat not of tales.
That fellow that grins here or yells,
I myself shall hurt him full sore.

ANNAS:

Ye shall set him full sore, what fool will unease you;
If he like not your lordship, that lad, shall ye make him,
As a peerless prince full promptly to please you,
Or as dreadful duke with dints shall ye take him.

CAYPHAS:

Yea, in faith, ye have force for to fear him;
Through your manhood and might he is marred;
No chivalrous chieftain may cheer him,
For that churl, his comfort is hard
      And wasted;
In pining pain is he barred.

ANNAS:

Yea, and with scathe of skelps ill scarred,
From the time that your wrath he has tasted.

PILATE:

Now sure, as meseems, who so seriously sought you,
Your praising is profitable, ye prelates of peace.
Gramercy for your good word; ungain shall it not you
That ye will say the sooth, and for no subject cease.

CAYPHAS:

Else were it pity we appeared in this press.
But see how your knights come at hand.

ANNAS:

Yea, my lord, that lovest no lies,
I can tell you, there betide some tidings
      Full sad.

PILATE:

See, they bring yon brat in a band.
We shall hear now hastily at hand
What unhap before Herod he had.

FIRST KNIGHT:

Hail, loveliest lord that ever law led yet;
Hail, seemliest sire on every side;
Hail, stateliest in stead in strength that is stead yet;
Hail, liberal; hail, lusty, to lords allied!

PILATE:

Welcome. What tidings this tide?
Let no language lightly now let you.

SECOND KNIGHT:

Sir Herod (it is not to hide)
As his good friend with grace did he greet you,
        For ever.
In what manner soe'er he may meet you,
By himself full soon will he set you.
And says that ye shall not dissever.

PILATE:

I thank him full throughly, and say him the same.
But what marvellous matters did this minion there tell?

FIRST KNIGHT:

For all the lord's language his lips, sir, were lame,
For any asking in that space no speech would he spill,
But dumb as a door did he dwell.
Thus no fault in him did he find,
For his deeds to deem him to quell,
Nor in bands him bitterly to bind,
And thus
He sent him to yourself, and assigned
That we, your knights, should be cleanly inclined
And quick with him to you to truss.

PILATE:

Sirs, hearken, Hear ye not what we have upon hand?
Lo, how these knights speak who to the king fared.
Sir Herod, they say, no fault in me found;

He fastens me in friendship, so friendly he fared.
Moreover, he spake and not spared
Full gently to Jesus that Jew;
And then to these knights here declared
How faults in him he found he but few
　　　To die.
He tested him, I tell you for true,
For to fright him he deemed undue;
And, sirs, so soothly say I.

CAYPHAS:
Sir Pilate our prince, we prelates now pray you,
Since Herod tried no further this false one to slay,
Receive in your hall these sayings I say you;
Bring him to the bar; at his beard we shall bay.

ANNAS:
Yea; for if we wend thus by wiles away,
I wot well he works us some wonder.
Our company he mars all he may;
With his sayings he sets them asunder
　　　In sin.
With his bluster he breeds many a blunder.
While ye have him, now hold him well under;
We shall curse him all way if he win.

CAYPHAS:
Sir, no time now to tarry this traitor to test;
Against Caesar himself he speaks and he says
All the wights in this world work in waste
That take him any tribute; thus his teaching bewrays.
Yet further he feigns such affrays,
And says that himself is God's son.
And, sir, our law alleges and lays
The felon in whom falsehood is found
　　　Should be slain.

PILATE:
For no shame him to slight will we shun.

ANNAS:

Sir, witness of these words may be won,
That will tell this is true, and not feign.

CAYPHAS:

I can reckon a rabble of fellows full right,
Of pert men in presence from this place ere I pass,
That will witness, I warrant, the words of this wight,
How wickedly wrought this wretch ever has . . .
Simon, Yarus and Judas,
Dathan and Gamaliell,
Nephtalim, Levi and Lucas,
And Amys these matters can tell
        Together;
These tales for true they can tell
Of this liar that false is and fell
And in alleging our laws full lither.

PILATE:

Ah tush for your tales! They touch not the intent.
These witnesses, I warrant, that to witness ye wage,
Some hatred in their hearts against him have lent,
And purpose by this process to put down this page.

CAYPHAS:

Sir, in faith it befits us not false to allege.
They are trusty and true men, we tell you.

PILATE:

Your swearing, sirs, swiftly assuage;
Mix no more in these matters, I will you
        And charge.

ANNAS:

Sir, despise not this speech that we spell you.

PILATE:

If ye feign such false frauds, I shall fell you,
For I like not this language so large.

CAYPHAS:
Our language is large, unless you will relieve us.
But we both beseech you, bring him to the bar.
What points we put forth, let your presence approve us;
You shall hear how he moves out of order afar.

PILATE:
Yea, but be wise, witty and wary.

ANNAS:
Sir, dread ye not, for nothing we fear him.
Fetch him; he is not right far.
Go, bedell; bestir thee about him.

BEADLE:
I am here,
My lord, for to lead him or lout him,
Unclothe him or clap him and clout him;
If ye bid, I obedient appear.
Sir knights, ye are commanded with this caitiff to care,
And bring him to bar, for so my lord bade.

FIRST KNIGHT:
Is this thy message?

BEADLE:
                Yea, sir.

FIRST KNIGHT:
                      Then move you no more,
For we are light for to leap and bring forth this lad.

SECOND KNIGHT:
Now step forth; in strife thou'rt bested;
Full ill, I uphold, has thee happed.

FIRST KNIGHT:
O man, thy mind is full mad,

In our clutch to be clouted and clapped
And closed.

SECOND KNIGHT:
Ye be lashed, slashed and lapped.

FIRST KNIGHT:
Yea, routed, rushed and rapped.
Thus thy name with annoy shall be noised.

SECOND KNIGHT:
Lo, this fellow, my sovereign, for which same ye sent.

PILATE:
Well, stir not from that stead, but stand still there.
Lest he shape some shrewdness in shame be he shent,
And I will try in faith to taste of his fare.

CAYPHAS:
Out, out! Stand I may not, so I stare.

ANNAS:
Ha, haro! for this traitor with pain.

PILATE:
Say, fellows, why roar you so there?
Are ye mad, or witless, I ween?
What ails you?

CAYPHAS:
Out! That such a sight should be seen.

ANNAS:
Yea, alas! We are conquered clean.

PILATE:
What, are ye fond, or your force fails you?

CAYPHAS:

Ah sir, saw ye not this sight, how the shafts shook,
And the banners to this beggar they bowed all abroad?

ANNAS:

Yea, those cursed knights by craft let them crook,
To worship this warlock whom they have in ward.

PILATE:

Was it truly done this, indeed?

CAYPHAS:

Yea, yea, sir; ourselves we it saw.

PILATE:

Bah, spit on them! Ill might they speed.
Say, dastards—the devil with you go—
How dare ye
These banners that broadly should blow
Let bow to this lurdan so low?
False fellows, with falsehood how fare ye?

THIRD KNIGHT:

We beseech you and the seniours who sit by your side,
With none of our governance be grieved so ill;
For it lay not in our lot these lances to guide,
And this work that we wrought, it was not our will.

PILATE:

Thou liest—hearest thou, lurdan?—full ill;
Well ye know it, if ye would admit.

FOURTH KNIGHT:

Sir, our strength might not steady them still;
They yielded for aught we could hold
With our might.

FIFTH KNIGHT:
For all our force, faith, did they fold,
As to worship this warlock they would,
And it seemed to us that was not right.

CAYPHAS:
Ah, liars unloyal, full false is your fable;
This fellow has fooled you to trust to his tale.

SIXTH KNIGHT:
You may say what you will, but these staves to hold stable
What fellow tries force, full foul shall he fail.

ANNAS:
Thou art doggedly dastard, by the devil's nail.
Ah, henheart, ill hap may you have.

PILATE:
For a whip how he whined and did wail;
Yet no lash to this lurdan he gave.
Foul fall you!

THIRD KNIGHT:
Sir, no trickery we cause in this case.

CAYPHAS:
Yet you sit here in shameless disgrace.
Now curst clumsy caitiffs, I call you.

FOURTH KNIGHT:
Since you like not, my lord, our language to love,
Bring in now the biggest men that bide in his land
Properly in your presence their power to prove,
And see if they yield when they have them in hand

PILATE:
Now ye fear most foully that ever I found;
Fie now on your faint hearts for fear.

Stir thee; no longer there stand,
Thou beadle; this bidword go bear
  All around.
The strongest of all men of war
And the stoutest these standards to bear,
Hither blithely bid them to be bound.

BEADLE:

My sovereign, full soon shall I serve thee, and so
I shall bring to these banners right big men and strong.
A company of knaves in this country I know
That are sturdy and stout, and to such will I go.
Say, ye lads both lusty and strong,
Ye must pass to Sir Pilate a pace.

FIRST SOLDIER:

If we work not his will it were wrong;
We are ready to run in a race
  Strong and stark.

BEADLE:

Then stay not, but step on apace,
And follow me fast to his face.

SECOND SOLDIER:

Lead on now; we like well this lark.

BEADLE:

Lord, here be the biggest bairns that bide in this bound,
Most stately and strong, if with strength they be strained.
Believe me, I lie not; to look this land round,
They're the mightiest men who have manhood attained.

PILATE:

Wot you well, or else hast thou weened?

BEADLE:

Sir, I wot well, without words more.

PILATE:
In thy tale be not tainted nor feigned.

BEADLE:
Why, no, sir; why should I be so?

PILATE:
Well, then;
We shall test ere they travel us fro.
To what game they begin them to go,
Sir Cayphas, declare them you can.

CAYPHAS:
Ye lusty lads, list as I bid you. Prepare;
Shape you to those shafts that shine there so plain.
If you bairns bow the breadth of a hair,
Ye are put to perpetual pain.

FIRST SOLDIER:
I shall hold it as straight as a line.

ANNAS:
Whoso shakes, shame on him depends.

SECOND SOLDIER:
Aye, certain. I say as for mine,
When it settles or sadly descends
Where I stand,
When it wavers or wrongly it wends,
Or bursts, breaks, or bends,
Why then, let them hack off my hand.

PILATE:
Sirs, watch on these wights, that no wiles may be
wrought.
They are burly and broad; their boasts they have blown.

ANNAS:

To name that now, sir, it needs right nought;
For who cursedly quits him, it soon shall be known.

CAYPHAS:

Yea, that dastard to death shall be drawn;
Whoso fails, he foully shall fall.

PILATE:

Now, knights, since 'tis past the cockcrow,
Have him hence with haste from this hall
      His ways.
So, smartly step up to this stall;
Make cry, and carefully call,
Even as Sir Anna he says.

ANNAS:

Oyez!
Jesus thou descendant of Duke Jacob's kin,
Thou ne'erthrive of Nazareth, now named is thy name.
All men who accuse thee, we bid them come in,
And answer thine accusers; defend now thy fame.

BEADLE:
Judicatur Jesus.

CAYPHAS:

Ha, out! What disgrace, to our shame.
This is wrested all wrong, as I ween.

ANNAS:

For all their boast, these boys were to blame.

PILATE:

Such a sight was never yet seen.
      Come sit.
My comfort was caught from me clean.

Up I start; I might not abstain
To worship in work and in wit.

CAYPHAS:

Much marvelled we both what moved you in mind
In reverence of this ribald so rudely to rise.

PILATE:

I was past all my power, though I pained me and pined;
I wrought not as I would, in no manner of wise.
Sirs, heed well my speech, I advise.
Quickly his ways let him wend.
Thus my doom will I duly devise.
For I fear, in faith, him to offend
        By lights.

ANNAS:

Then our laws were drawn to an end,
To his tales if you truly attend;
For by witchcraft he worked on these wights.

CAYPHAS:

By his sorcery, sir—yourself the truth saw—
He charmed our chevaliers and myself enchanted.
To reverence him royally we rose all in a row;
Doubtless we endure not of this dastard to be daunted.

PILATE:

Why, what harms has this noble here haunted?
I know to convict him no cause.

ANNAS:

To all men he God's son him granted,
And lists not to live by our laws.

PILATE:

                    Say, man,
Conceive you not what cumbersome clause

That this clergy accusing you knows?
Speak; excuse thyself, if thou can.

JESUS:

Every man has a mouth that is made upon mould,
In weal and in woe to wield at his will.
If he govern it goodly, like as God would,
For his spiritual speech he needs not to spill;
And what man shall govern it ill,
Full unhandy and ill shall he hap.
For each tale unto us that you tell
You account shall; you cannot escape.

PILATE:

Sirs mine,

Ye found, in faith, all his design;
For in this lad no lies can I trap,
Nor no point to put him to pine.

CAYPHAS:

Without cause, sir, we come not, this churl to accuse him;
That will we ye wit, as well is worthy.

PILATE:

Now I record well the right; ye will no sooner refuse him
Till he be driven to his death and doomed to die.
But take him to you thereby,
And like as your law will decide,
Doom ye his body to abide.

ANNAS:

O Sir Pilate without any peer,
    Now nay;
Ye wot well (no doubt can appear)
We may not, not all of us here,
Slay no man, to you truth to say.

PILATE:

Shall I doom him to death, not deserving in deed?
But I have heard wholly why in heart ye him hate.
He is faultless, in faith, and so God might me speed,
I grant him my good will to gang on his gate.

CAYPHAS:

Not so, sir; for well ye it wot,
To be king he claimeth with crown.
Who so stoutly will step to that state,
You should doom, sir, to be set down
    And dead.

PILATE:

Sir, truly that touches to treason,
And ere I remove he shall rue that reason,
Ere I stalk or stir from this stead.
Sir knights that are comely, take this caitiff in keeping;
Skelp him with scourges and scathe him full sore;
Wrest him and wring him till for woe he is weeping,
And then bring him before us as he was before.

FIRST KNIGHT:

He may ban the time that he was born;
Soon shall he be served as ye bade us.

ANNAS:

Come, whip off his weeds that are worn.

SECOND KNIGHT:

All ready, sir, we have arrayed us;
    Have done.
For this brawler soon ready we have made us,
As Sir Pilate has properly prayed us.

THIRD KNIGHT:

We shall set to him seriously anon.

FOURTH KNIGHT:
Let us get off his gear, God give him ill grace.

FIRST KNIGHT:
They are stripped off soon, lo, take there his trashes.

THIRD KNIGHT:
Now knit him in this cord.

SECOND KNIGHT:
                              I am keen in this case.

FOURTH KNIGHT:
He is bound fast; now beat on with bitter brashes.
Go on; leap, hear ye, lordings, with lashes;
And enforce we this fellow to flay him.

SECOND KNIGHT:
Let us drive to him dreadfully with dashes;
All red with our rods we array him
        And rend him.

THIRD KNIGHT:
For my part, I am prompt for to pay him.

FOURTH KNIGHT:
Yea, send him sorrow; assay him.

FIRST KNIGHT:
Take him till I have time to attend him.

SECOND KNIGHT:
Swing to this pillar; too swiftly he sweats.

THIRD KNIGHT:
Sweat may this swain for weight of our swaps.

FOURTH KNIGHT:
Rush on this ribald and rapidly revive.

FIRST KNIGHT:
Revive him I rede you, with routs and with raps.

SECOND KNIGHT:
For all our annoying, this niggard he naps.

THIRD KNIGHT:
We shall wake him with wind of our whips.

FOURTH KNIGHT:
Now fling to this flatterer with flaps.

FIRST KNIGHT:
I shall heartily hit on his hips
       And haunch.

SECOND KNIGHT:
From our skelps not scatheless he skips.

THIRD KNIGHT:
Yet list he not lift up his lips,
And pray us have pity on his paunch.

FOURTH KNIGHT:
To have pity on his paunch he proffers no prayer.

FIRST KNIGHT:
Lord, how likest thou this lark, and this lore that we learn
    you?

SECOND KNIGHT:
Lo, I pull at his pelt; I am a proud payer.

THIRD KNIGHT:
Thus your cloak shall we clout, to cleanse you and clear
    you.

FOURTH KNIGHT:
I am strong in this strife for to stir you.

FIRST KNIGHT:
Thus with chops this churl shall we chastise.

SECOND KNIGHT:
I trow with this trace we shall tear you.

THIRD KNIGHT:
All thine untrue teachings thus taste I,
          Fool arrant.

FOURTH KNIGHT:
I think I be hardy and hasty.

FIRST KNIGHT:
I wot well my weapon not waste.

SECOND KNIGHT:
He swoons or he faints soon, I warrant.

THIRD KNIGHT:
Let us loose him lightly; come, lay on your hands.

FOURTH KNIGHT:
Yea; for if he die for this deed, undone are we all.

FIRST KNIGHT:
Now unbound is this boy, and unbraced are his hands.

SECOND KNIGHT:
O fool, how fares thou now, foul might thou fall?

THIRD KNIGHT:
Now because he our king did him call,
We will kindly him crown with a briar.

FOURTH KNIGHT:
Yea, but first this purple and pall
And this worthy weed shall he wear,
 For scorn.

FIRST KNIGHT:
I am proud at this point to appear.

SECOND KNIGHT:
Let us clothe him in these clothes all clear,
As a lord that his lordship has lorn.

THIRD KNIGHT:
'Twill be long ere thou meet with such men as thou met
 with this morn.

FOURTH KNIGHT:
Do set him in this seat, as a seemly in hall.

FIRST KNIGHT:
Now press to him tightly with this thick thorn.

SECOND KNIGHT:
Lo, it holds so to his head that the brains out fall.

THIRD KNIGHT:
Thus we teach him to temper his tales;
His brain begins for to bleed.

FOURTH KNIGHT:
Yea, his blunders brought him to these bales.
Now reach him a rush or a reed
 So round;
For his sceptre it serves indeed.

FIRST KNIGHT:
Yea, it is good enough in this need.
Let us goodly him greet on this ground.

Ave, right royal, and Rex Judeorum!
Hail, comely king, that no kingdom has kenned.
Hail, duke doughty; thy deeds are dumb.
Hail, man unmighty thy means to mend.

THIRD KNIGHT:
Hail, lord without land to command.
Hail, king; hail, fool feeble of hand.

FOURTH KNIGHT:
Hail, fool with no force to defend.
Hail, strong man that may not well stand
        To strive.

FIRST KNIGHT:
Ho, harlot; here, heave up thy hand,
And us all that in worship are working,
Thank us. And ill might thou thrive.

SECOND KNIGHT:
So; let us lead him now lively, and linger no longer.
To Sir Pilate the prince our pride will we praise.

THIRD KNIGHT:
Yea; he may sing ere he sleep for sorrow and anger,
For many dread deeds has he done in his days.

FOURTH KNIGHT:
Now lightly let us wend on our ways;
Let's truss us; no time is to tarry.

FIRST KNIGHT:
My lord, will ye list to our lays?
Here this boy is you bade us go harry
        With blows.
We are cumbered his corse for to carry.
Many wights on him wonder and worry.
Lo, his flesh, how its beatings it shows.

PILATE:

Well, bring him before us. Ah, he blushes all blue.
I suppose of his saying he'll cease evermore.
Sirs, look here on high and see: ECCE HOMO.
Thus beaten and bound and brought you before.
Methinks that it suits him full sore;
For his guilt on this ground he is grieved.
. . . [*A leaf is lost here.*[1]]
*And the measure that now I shall move,
It may move you to mercy the more
          And grace.
For to doom him to death I deplore;
I would fain set him free from this place.
Your custom hath been to let go
Some felon to freedom this day.

CAYPHAS:

Barabbas in prison lies low;
At this feast now release him, we pray.

PILATE:

A rebel still raging to slay?
Would ye rather that I should release
This Jesus?

ALL:

               Barabbas, we say.

PILATE:

                         Will ye cease?
None is heard, for each howleth so loud.

ALL:

Not this man; Barabbas.

---

[1] *-*. The matter of this lost leaf is so essential to the action
that I have attempted to supply the sense of the missing lines.—
J. S. P.

PILATE:

Ho, peace!
Ye clamour and call in a crowd.
If this is your will so to be,
For Jesus now what is your mind?
His evil deeds done show to me,
For in him no fault can I find;
Good he ever hath done to mankind.

CAYPHAS:

Away with him now; let him die.

PILATE:

Shall I scourge him again, and unbind?

ALL:

Nay; crucify him. Crucify.
If thou loose him, thou art not Caesar's friend.

PILATE:

On you be his blood, then, say I.

CAYPHAS:

On us be his blood. Make an end.

ALL:

Crucify!

PILATE:

Then since your will I may not bend,
All my part in his bloodshed I henceforth deny.*
For properly by this process I will prove
I had no force from this fellowship this man to defend.

BEADLE:

Here is all, sir, for which you did send.
Will you wash while the water is hot?

* PILATE:
Bear witness, all ye that are here.
From the guilt of his blood I am clear,
For innocent he.

CAYPHAS:
On us that same blood without fear,
And our children to come, let it be.

ALL:
On us and our sons let it be. *

PILATE:
From Barabbas his bonds now unbend;
With grace let him gang on his gate
    Where you will.

BARABBAS:
Ye worthy men goodly and great,
God increase all your comely estate,
For the grace ye have granted me still.

PILATE:
Hear the judgement of Jesus, all Jews in this stead.
Crucify him on a cross, and on Calvary him kill.
I condemn him this day to die this same death;
Therefore hang him on high upon that high hill.
And on either side of him I will
That a harlot ye hang in this haste;
Methinks it both reason and skill
That amidst, since his malice is most,
    Ye hang him.
Then torment him, some torture to taste.
More words I will not now waste;
But stay not, to death till ye bring him.

CAYPHAS:
Sir, it seems in our sight that is soberly said.
Now, knights that are cunning, with this catiff go fare;
The life of this looseling at your liking is laid.

FIRST KNIGHT:
Let us alone, lord, and learn us no more.
Sirs, set to him sadly and sore.
Let the cords round his body be cast.

SECOND KNIGHT:
Let us bind him in bands all bare.

THIRD KNIGHT:
Here is one; full long will it last.

FOURTH KNIGHT:
Lay on hands here.

FIFTH KNIGHT:
I pull till my power is past.
Now fast is he, fellows, full fast.
Let us stir us; we may not long stand here.

ANNAS:
Draw him fast; hence deliver you; have done.
Go, see him to death without longer delay;
For dead must he needs be by noon.
All mirth must we move tomorrow that we may;
It is soothly our great Sabbath day.
No dead bodies unburied shall be.

SIXTH KNIGHT:
We see well the truth that ye say.
We shall trail him fast to his tree,
        Thus talking.

FOURTH KNIGHT:
Farewell; now quickly wend we.

PILATE:
Now sure, ye are a brave company.
Forth with a wild vengeance be walking.

heavy alliteration

THE CRUCIFIXION

York Butchers' Play

JESUS:

> Thou man that amiss here has meant,
> To me tent entirely now take
> On the rood am I ragged and rent,
> Thou sinful of soul, for thy sake.
> For thy misdeed amends will I make;
> I bide here, my back to bend low.
> This woe for thy trespass I take
> Who could thee more kindliness show
>   Than I?
> Thus for thy good
> I shed my blood.
> Man, mend thy mood
> For full bitter thy bliss must I buy.

MARY:

> Alas for my sweet son, I say,
> That doleful to death here is dight.
> Alas, for full lovely he lay
> In my womb, this most wonderful wight.
> Alas, that this blossom so bright
> Untruly is tugged to this tree.
>   Alas!
> My Lord, my life,
> With full great grief
> Hangs as a thief.
> Alas, he did never trespass.

211

JESUS:

> Thou woman, no more weep; be still;
> For me may thou nothing amend.
> To work out my Father's good will,
> For all mankind my body I bend.

MARY:

> Alas, that thou mayest not stay.
> How should I not weep for thy woe?
> Grief takes all my comfort away.
> Alas, must we part us in two
>> For ever?

JESUS:

> Woman, instead of me,
> Lo, John thy son shall be.
> John, see to thy mother free;
> For my sake do thy devoir.

MARY:

> Alas, son! I sorrow on height
> Would that I were closed in clay,
> A sword of such sorrow doth smite.
> The death might I die this day.

JOHN:

> Ah, mother, so shall you not say.
> I pray you, even here be at peace.
> For with all the might that I may
> Your comfort I cast to increase
>> Indeed.
> Your son am I,
> Lo, here ready
> And now thereby
> I pray you hence for to speed.

MARY:

> My cry for to cease, or to stir,
> How can I, such sight when I see?

My son, that is worthy and dear,
Thus doleful a death for to die.

JOHN:

Ah mother dear, cease this misery.
Your mourning, it may not amend.

MARY CLEOPAS:

Ah Mary, take trust unto me,
For succour to thee will he send
    This tide.

JOHN:

Fair mother, fast
Hence let us cast.

MARY:

Till he be passed
Will I be here near him to bide.

JESUS:

With bitterest bale have I bought
Thus, man, thy misdeeds to amend.
On me for to look stay thou not
How humbly my body I bend.
No wight in this wide world would ween
What sorrow I suffer for thy sake.
Man, my care for thy kind to be seen,
True tent unto me shalt thou take,
    And trust.
For foxes their dens have they,
Birds have their nests so gay,
But the Son of Man this day
Has not where his head he may rest.

THIEF ON LEFT:

If thou be God's son so free,
Why hangest thou thus on this hill?

To save now thyself let us see,
And us, that speed so to spill.

THIEF ON RIGHT:

Man, stint of thy sound and be still,
For doubtless thy God dreadest thou not.
Full well are we worthy of ill;
Unwisely much wrong have we wrought,
                    I wis.
No ill did he,
Thus for to die.
Lord, have mind of me,
When thou art come to thy bliss.

JESUS:

For sooth, son, to thee shall I say,
Since thou from thy folly wilt fall,
With me shalt thou dwell now this day
In paradise place principal.
Heloy! Heloy!
My God, my God full free,
Lama Sabatanye,
Wherefore forsook thou me
                    In care?
And I did never ill,
This death for to endure—
But be it at thy will.
Ah! I thirst sore.

BOY:

A drink shall I dress thee indeed,
A draught that is daintily dight.
Full fast shall I spring for to speed,
I hope I shall hold what I plight.

CAYPHAS:

Sir Pilate that most is of might,
Hark! "Hely," I now heard him cry.
He looks for that worthiest wight,

In haste for to help him on high
    In his need.

PILATE:

If he do so,
He shall have woe.

ANNAS:

He were our foe
If he dress him to do us that deed.

BOY:

That deed for to dress if he do,
For sure he shall rue it full sore.
Ne'ertheless, if he like it not, lo,
Full soon may he cover that care.
Now, sweet sir, your will if it were,
A draught here of drink have I dressed.
No need for expense that ye spare
But boldly bib it for the best.
      For why?
Vinegar and gall
Are mixed withal.
Drink it ye shall.
Your lips, I hold them full dry.

JESUS:

Thy drink, it shall do me no harm;
Know well, I will take of it none.
Now, Father who all things didst form,
To thy most might I make me my moan.
Thy will have I wrought all alone,
Thus ragged and rent on this rood.
Thus doleful to death am I done.
Forgive them, by grace that is good;
      They knew not what it was.
My Father, hear my boon
For now all things are done.

My spirit to thee right soon
Commend I, *IN MANUS TUAS.*

MARY:

Now, dear son Jesus so gentle,
Since my heart is as heavy as lead,
One word would I wit ere you went. . . .
Alas! Now my dear son is dead,
Full ruefully rent and forspent.
Alas, for my darling so dear!

JOHN:

Ah, mother, now hold up thy head,
And sigh not with sorrows severe,
    I pray.

MARY CLEOPAS:

It grieves her heart
To see him part.
Hence let us start.
This mourning no help can convey.

CAYPHAS:

Sir Pilate, perceive you, I pray;
Our customs to keep well ye can.
Tomorrow is our dear Sabbath day;
Of mirth must we move every man.
These warlocks are waxen full wan,
And needs now they buried be.
Deliver those dead, sir, and then
Shall we go to our solemnity
    Indeed.

PILATE:

That shall I do
In words full few.
Sir knights, go to;

To yon harlots now handily take heed.
Those caitiffs, kill them with the knife.
Deliver; have done; see them dead.

KNIGHT:

My lord, I shall lengthen their life,
So that none of them more shall bite bread.

PILATE:

Sir Longeus, step forth in this stead;
This spear, lo, hold here in thy hand.
To Jesus now set forth with speed,
And stay not till stiffly thou stand.
In Jesus' side
Shove it this tide.
No longer bide,
But go thou directly at hand.

LONGEUS:

O maker unmade, full of might,
O Jesus so gentle and kind,
That sudden has sent me my sight—
Lord, loving to thee be assigned.
On rood thou art ragged and rent,
Mankind to amend when amiss.
Full spitefully spilt is and spent
Thy blood, Lord, to bring us to bliss
　　　Full free.
Ah mercy, my succour;
Mercy, my treasure;
Mercy, my Saviour.
Thy mercy be marked in me.

CENTURION:

O wonderful worker, I wis.
The weather is waxed full wan.
True token I trow that it is,
That mercy is meant unto man.
No cause in this case could they know,

That dolefully doomed him amain,
To lose thus his life by their law
                    Unright.
Truly I say,
God's very son
Was he this day,
That doleful to death thus is dight.

JOSEPH OF ARIMATHEA:

That true lord aye lasting in land,
Sir Pilate, now present in press,
May He save you by sea and by sand,
And all that are duly on dais.

PILATE:

Joseph—this is truly no lies—
To me art thou welcome, I wis.
Now tell me the truth ere thou cease,
Thy worthy good will what it is,
                    Anon.

JOSEPH:

To thee I pray,
Give me today
Jesus' body
Under favour to bury it alone.

PILATE:

Sir Joseph, I grant thee that gest.
I grudge not to get him in grave.
Deliver: have done he were dressed;
And seek, sir, our Sabbath to save.

JOSEPH:

With hands and with heart that I have,
I thank thee in faith for my friend.
God keep thee, thy comfort to crave,
For swiftly my way will I wend
                    On high.

To do that deed,
He be my speed
Whose arms were spread,
Mankind by his blood for to buy.

NICHODEMUS:

Well met, sir. I moved in my thought
For Jesus that judged was amiss.
For licence you laboured and sought
To bury his body from rood.

JOSEPH:

Full mildly that matter I would,
And that for to do will I dress.

NICHODEMUS:

Together I would that we went,
And stay not for more nor for less.
For why?
Our friend was he,
Faithful and free.

JOSEPH:

Therefore go we,
To bury that body on high.
Let each man now mark in his mind,
To see here this sorrowful sight
No falseness in him could they find,
That doleful to death thus is dight.

NICHODEMUS:

He was aye a full worthy wight,
Now blemished and bloody and bruised.

JOSEPH:

Yea, since that he showed not his might,
Full falsely our friend they abused,
I ween.

Both back and side,
His wounds are wide;
Therefore this tide
Take we now him down, us between.

NICHODEMUS:

Between us now take we him down,
And lay him by length on this land.

JOSEPH:

This reverend and rich of renown,
Let us hold him and lift him with hand.
A grave have I late here ordained,
That never was in need; 'tis new.

NICHODEMUS:

To this corpse it is comely consigned,
To dress him with deeds full due,
                This day.

JOSEPH:

A sudary,
Lo, here have I;
Wind him thereby
And soon shall we grave him, I say.

NICHODEMUS:

In ground let us grave him, and go;
Come, swift let us lay him alone.
Now, Saviour of me and of mo,
Keep us here in cleanness each gone.

JOSEPH:

To thy mercy now make I my moan
As Saviour by sea and by sand;
So guide me that grief be all gone,
To live long and true in this land
                At ease.

NICHODEMUS:

>Rich ointments have I
>Brought for this fair body.
>I anoint thee thereby
>With myrrh and aloes.

JOSEPH:

>This deed, it is done every deal,
>And well wrought this work is, I wis.
>To thee, King, on knees here I kneel,
>That closely thou keep me in bliss.

NICHODEMUS:

>He called me full clear to be his,
>One night when I nighed him full near.
>Have mind, Lord, and mend where I miss.
>For done are our deeds here full dear,
>>This tide.

JOSEPH:

>This lord so good
>That shed his blood,
>Mend he your mood,
>And bring in his bliss to abide.

17

THE HARROWING OF HELL

York Saddlers' Play

JESUS:

> Man on mould, be meek to me,
> And have thy maker in thy mind,
> And think how I have borne for thee,
> With peerless pains for to be pined.
> The promise of my Father free
> Have I fulfilled, as folk may find.
> Therefore about now will I be
> Those I have brought for to unbind.
> The fiend with fraud did gain
> Through fruit of earthly food;
> I have them gotten again
> Through buying with my blood.
> And so I shall that state restore
> From which the fiend fell for sin;
> There shall mankind dwell evermore.
> In bliss that never shall decline.
> All that in work my workmen were,
> Out of their woe I will them win,
> And some sign shall I send before
> Of grace to make their games begin.
> A light I will they have,
> To shew I shall come soon.
> My body bides in grave
> Till all these deeds be done.
> My Father ordained on this wise,
> After his will that I should wend

For to fulfil the prophecies,
And I as spake my solace to spend.
My friends that on me in faith relies
Now from their foes I shall defend,
And on the third day right uprise,
And so to heaven I shall ascend.
Then shall I come again,
To judge both good and ill,
To endless joy or pain;
Thus is my Father's will.

ADAM:

My brethren, hearken to me here.
Such hope of health we never had.
Four thousand and six hundred year
Have we been held here in this stead.
Now see I sign of solace clear,
A glorious gleam to make us glad;
Wherefore I hope our health is near,
And soon shall cease our sorrows sad.

EVA:

Adam, my husband free,
This means solace certain;
Such light shall on us be
In Paradise full plain.

ISAIAH:

Adam, we shall well understand.
I, Ysasias, whom God did send,
I preached in Nepthalim's fair land
And Zabulon even to my end.
I spake of folk in darkness set,
And said a light should on them land.
Thus learned I then while living yet,
Now see I God the same did send;
This light comes all of Christ,
That seed to save us now.

Thus is my point published;
But Symeon, what sayest thou?

SYMEON:

Yes; my tale of wonders now I tell,
For in this Temple his friends me found;
I had delight with him to deal,
And held him homely in my hand.
I said, "Lord, let thy servant leal
Pass now in peace to lasting life,
For now myself has seen thy heal
I list no longer live in land."
This light thou hast purveyed
To folks that live on mould;
The same as I then said
I see fulfilled indeed.

JOHN BAPTIST:

As voice crying I told all lands
The ways of Christ, as well I can.
I baptised him with both my hands,
Even in the flood of flowing Jordan.
The Holy Ghost did from heaven descend
As a white dove down on him then;
The Father's voice, my mirth to mend
Was made to me even as man—
"This is my son," He said,
"In whom I am pleased full well."
His light is on us laid;
He comes our cares to heal.

MOYSES:

Of that same light learning have I.
To me Moyses he mustered his might,
And also to another, Hely,
When we were on a hill on height.
White as the snow was his body,

And his face like to the sun to sight.
No man on mould was so mighty
Fully to look against that light.
That same light see I now
Shining on us certain;
Wherefore truly I trow
We shall soon pass from pain.

FIRST DEVIL:

Help, Belzabub, to bind these boys!
Such harrow was never heard in hell.

SECOND DEVIL:

Why roarest thou so, Rybald?
What may betide? Canst thou ought say?

FIRST DEVIL:

What! Hearest thou not this ugly noise?
These lurdans that in Limbo dwell,
They make meaning of many joys,
And muster them great mirth to tell.

SECOND DEVIL:

Mirth?
Nay, nay; that point is past;
More help shall they not have.

FIRST DEVIL:

They cry on Christ full fast,
And say he shall them save.

BELZABUB:

Yea, if he save them not, we shall,
For they are sparred in special space;
While I am prince and principal
Shall they not pass out of this place.
Call up Astrot and Anabal,
To give their counsel in this case,

Baal, Berit and Belial,
To mar them that such masteries make.
Say to Satan our sire,
And bid them bring also,
Lucifer lovely to see.

FIRST DEVIL:

All ready, lord, I go.

JESUS:

ATTOLLITE, PORTAS, PRINCIPES.
Open up, ye princes of pains severe,
ET ELEVAMINI ETERNALES,
Your endless gates that ye have here.

SATAN:

What page is there that makes such press,
And calls him king of us all here?

DAVID:

When living learned I, without lies,
He is a king of virtues clear.
With him ye may not fight,
For he is king and conqueror.
A lord mickle of might,
And strong to strive with power,
In battle fierce to fight,
And worthy to win honour.

SATAN:

Honour? In the devil's way, for what deed?
All earthly men to me are thrall;
The lad that calls him lord indeed
Had never yet harbour, house nor hall.

FIRST DEVIL:

Hark, Belzabub! I have great dread,
For hideously I heard him call.

BELIAL:

> Ho! Spar our gates, ill might you all speed!
> And set forth watches on the wall.
> And if he call or cry,
> To make us more debate,
> Lay on him then hardily
> And make him gang his gate.

SATAN:

> Tell me what boy dare be so bold
> For dread to make such disarray.

FIRST DEVIL:

> It is the Jew that Judas sold
> To die the death, the other day.

SATAN:

> Out, out! This tale in time is told;
> This traitor crosses us alway.
> He shall be here full hard to hold;
> Look that he pass not, I thee pray.

SECOND DEVIL:

> Nay, nay; he shall not go
> Away ere I be aware.
> He shapes him to undo
> All Hell ere he go far.

SATAN:

> Nay, fainthearts; thereof shall he fail;
> For all his fare I him defy.
> I know his tricks from top to tail;
> He lives with gauds and guilery.
> Thereby he brought out of our bail
> Now lately, Lazar of Betannye.
> Therefore I gave the Jews counsel
> That they should all way make him die.
> I entered in Judas

That purpose to fulfil;
Therefore his hire he has,
Always to dwell here still.

BELZABUB:

Sir Satan, since we hear thee say
That thou and the Jews did all assent,
And knew he won Lazar away,
That to us was brought for to tent,
Trust thou then that thou mar him may
To muster might as he has meant?
If he deprive us of our prey,
We would ye wit well where they went.

SATAN:

I bid you be no more abashed,
But boldly bring your armour soon,
With tools on which ye trust,
And ding that dastard down.

JESUS:

PRINCIPES, PORTA TOLLITE;
Undo your gates, ye princes of pride,
ET INTROIBIT REX GLORIE,
The king of bliss comes in this tide.

SATAN:

Out, haro! What harlot here is he,
That says his kingdom shall be cried?

DAVID:

That may thou in my Psalter see,
For that point of prophecy.
I said that he should break
Your bars and bands by name,
And on your works take wreak;
Now shall ye see the same.

JESUS:

> This stead shall stand no more, by token;
> Open up, and let my people pass.

FIRST DEVIL:

> Out! Behold, all our bailey is broken,
> And burst are all our bands of brass.
> Tell Lucifer all is unlocken.

BELZABUB:

> What then? Is Limbo lorn, alas?
> Make, Satan, help! We are forsaken.
> This work is worse than ever it was.

SATAN:

> I bade he should be bound,
> If he made masteries more;
> Go, strike him to the ground,
> And set him sad and sore.

BELZABUB:

> Yea, "set him sore"—that is soon said;
> But come thyself and serve him so.
> We may not bide his bitter blow;
> He will us mar, even were we mo.

SATAN:

> What, fainthearts? Wherefore are ye feared?
> Have ye no force to flit him fro?
> See quick that all my gear's prepared;
> Myself shall to that gadling go.
> Now, bel ami; abide,
> With all thy boastful cheer;
> And tell to me this tide
> What masteries make you here?

JESUS:

> I make no masteries but for mine;
> Them will I save, I say again.

You had no power them to pine
But as my gaoler for their gain.
Here have they sojourned, not as thine
But in thy ward, thou wottest well how.

SATAN:

Then what the devil didst thou since then,
Who ne'er came near them until now?

JESUS:

Now is the time certain
My Father ordained before,
That they should pass from pain
And dwell in mirth ever more.

SATAN:

Thy Father knew I well by sight;
He was a wight his meat to win;
And Mary I know, thy mother hight,
And the uttermost end of all thy kin.
Who made thee be so mickle of might?

JESUS:

Thou wicked fiend, let be thy din.
My Father dwells in heaven on height,
With bliss that never wanes therein.
His own Son I full well,
His promise to fulfil;
Together shall we dwell
Or sunder, when we will.

SATAN:

God's Son? Then shouldst thou be full glad;
After no chattels needs thou crave.
But thou hast lived aye like a lad,
And in sorrow as a simple knave.

JESUS:

That was for hearty love I had

Unto man's soul, it for to save,
And for to make thee mazed and mad.
And by that reason duly to have,
My Godhead did I hide
In Mary, mother mine,
That it should not be spied
By thee nor none of thine.

SATAN:

Ah! This would I were told in town.
So since thou sayest God is thy sire,
I shall thee prove by right reason
Thou movest thy men into the mire.
To break his bidding they were bound.
And since they did at thy desire,
From Paradise he put them down
Into hell here to have their hire.
And thyself day and night
Hast taught, all men among,
To do reason and right
And here workest thou all wrong.

JESUS:

I work not wrong, that shalt thou wit,
If I my men from woe will win.
My prophets plainly preached it,
All these matters that now begin.
They said that after my obit
To hell then I should enter in,
And save my servants from that pit
Where damned souls shall sit for sin.
And each true prophet's tale
Must be fulfilled in me;
I bought them by my bale,
And in bliss shall they be.

SATAN:

Now since thou wilt allege the laws,
Thou shalt be attainted ere we go.

For them that thou to witness draws,
Full even against thee will they show.
Salamon has said in his saw
That whoso enters hell within
Shall never come out, as clerks know,
And therefore, fellow, leave thy din.
Job, thy servant also,
Thus in his time did tell,
That neither friend nor foe
Should find release in hell.

JESUS:

He said full sooth, that shalt thou see,
That in hell may be no release,
But of that place then preached he
Where sinful care shall ever increase.
In that bale ever shalt thou be
Where sorrows sore shall never cease;
And that my folk therefrom were free,
Now shall they pass to the place of peace.
They were here with thy will
And so forth shall they wend,
And thyself shalt fulfil
Their woe without end.

SATAN:

Oho!
Then see I how thou movest along,
Some measure with thy malice to tell,
Since thou sayest all shall not gang,
But some shall alway with us dwell.

JESUS:

Yea, wit thou well, else were it wrong—
As cursed Cayne that slew Abell,
And all that haste themselves to hang,
As Judas and Archedefell,
Datan and Abiron
And all of their assent,

As tyrants every one
That me and mine torment.
All that list not to learn my lore
That I have left in land now new,
That is, my coming for to know
And to my sacrament pursue,
My death, my rising, read by row—
Who will not trust they are not true,
Unto my doom I shall them draw,
And judge them worse than any few.
And all that like to learn
My law and live thereby
Shall never have harms here
But weal, as is worthy.

SATAN:

Now here's my hand. I hold me glad
This plan will plain our profit save.
If this be sooth that thou hast said,
We shall have more than now we have.
This law that thou now late hast laid
I shall teach men not to allow;
If they take it, they be betrayed,
For I shall turn them soon, I trow.
I shall walk East and West,
And make them work worse far.

JESUS:

Nay, fiend, thou shalt be fast,
That thou shalt flit not far.

SATAN:

Fast! That were a foul reason!
Nay, bel ami, thou must be smit.

JESUS:

Michael, my angel, hither soon!
Fasten yon fiend, that he not flit.

And, devil, I command thee, go down
Into thy cell where thou shalt sit.

SATAN:

Out, ah, haro! Now help, Mahound!
Now wax I woe out of my wit.

BELZABUB:

Satan, this said we ere.
Now shalt thou feel thy fit.

SATAN:

Alas, for dole and care!
I sink into hell pit.

ADAM:

Ah, Jesu Lord, mickle is thy might
That meek art made in this manner,
Us for to help by promise plight
When I and she both forfeit were.
Here have we lived long without light
Four thousand and six hundred year;
Now see I by this solemn sight
How thy mercy has made us clear.

EVA:

Ah lord, we were worthy
More torments for to taste;
But mend us with mercy,
As thou of might art most.

JOHN BAPTIST:

Ah lord, I love thee inwardly,
That would make me thy messenger,
Thy coming on earth for to cry
And teach thy faith to all folk here;
And then before thee for to die
And bring thy bidding to them here,

That they should have thy help on high.
Now see I all thy points appear,
As David, prophet true,
Oft times told unto us;
Of this coming he knew,
And said it should be thus.

DAVID:

As I have said, yet say I so;
*NE DERELINQUAS, DOMINE
ANIMAM MEAM IN INFERNO:*
Leave not my soul, Lord, after thee
In deep hell where the damned shall go,
Nor suffer souls from thee to be,
The sorrow of them that dwell in woe
Aye full of filth and may not flee.

ADAM:

We thank his great goodness
Who fetched us from this place;
Make joy now more and less.

OMNES:

We laud God of his grace.

JESUS:

Adam and all my friends now here,
From all your foes come forth to me;
Ye shall be set in solace clear,
Where ye shall never sorrows see.
And Michael, my archangel dear,
Receive these souls all unto thee,
And lead them that they may appear
To Paradise in glad plenty.
Now to my grave I go,
Ready to rise upright;
And then fulfil I so
What I before have plight.

MICHAEL:

> Lord, wend we shall after thy law
> To solace sure at thy command.
> But that no devil's draught us draw
> Lord, bless us with thy holy hand.

JESUS:

> My blessing have ye all in row;
> I shall be with you where you wend.
> All loyal ones that love my law
> They shall be blessed without an end.

ADAM:

> To thee, Lord, be loving,
> That us hast won from woe
> For solace will we sing
> *LAVS TIBI DOMINO*
> > *CUM GLORIA.*

18

THE THREE MARIES

Cornish Cycle

> *Here shall come* MARY MAGDALENE, *and* MARY *says:*

MARY MAGDALENE:
> What shall I do, alas?
> My Lord is gone into the grave.
>   Three days have passed,
> And this is the day to see
> If he is risen again,
>   Risen again at last.

> *Then shall come* MARY, *mother of* JAMES, *and*
> MARY SALOME:

MARY, MOTHER OF JAMES:
> Much comfort he was to us;
> Alas, that we have seen
>   Such death and such pain.
> I will go see if he
> Who redeemed me by his death
>   Is risen again.

MARY SALOME:
> The third day is to-day,
> The day to go and see
>   If he is risen again.
> For the anguish that he had

There is always in my heart
This sorrow and pain.

Here MARY MAGDALENE *shall meet them.*

MARY MAGDALENE:

Women, all joy to you,
Both Mary, mother of James,
And Mary Salome too.
Yet sorrow is in my heart;
If the body of God be gone,
Where shall it be found anew?

MARY, MOTHER OF JAMES:

And so it is with me,
Such sorrow I have for him.
If he brings me no relief,
And will not comfort me,
I know not what I shall do.
My heart will break for grief.

MARY SALOME:

Sorrow is mine also;
My longing may he relieve,
To see him with my eyes.
As he is King of Kings,
Out of the grave to-day
I believe that he will rise.

MARY MAGDALENE:

Oh, let us hasten amain,
For I see the stone is moved
From the tomb away.
Lord, how will it be this night
If I know not whither is gone
The Prince of royalty?

MARY, MOTHER OF JAMES:

Ah, too long have we stayed,
My Lord is gone away,

Out of the tomb indeed.
Alas, my heart is sick,
For I know not when I shall see
The Lord who is my need.

MARY SALOME:

I know, and I believe
That he is risen again
This very day.
Yet how will it be with us
That we cannot find our Lord,
Now he is gone away?

ALL: (*singing*)

Alas, mourning I sing,
Mourning I call;
Our Lord is dead
That bought us all.

MARY MAGDALENE *weeps at the tomb.*

MARY MAGDALENE:

Alas, for sorrow and grief,
That my sweet Lord is dead,
Whom I saw crucified.
On his dear body he bore
Much pain without complaint,
And for his people died.

MARY, MOTHER OF JAMES:

I cannot see a sign
Of him on any side;
Alas, that he should depart!
I long to speak with him,
If but it were his will,
So heavy is my heart.

MARY SALOME:

And always in my heart

Are longing and such grief
　In piteous plight.
Alas, my Saviour dear,
That art so debonair
　And full of might.

ALL: (*singing*)

Alas, mourning I sing,
　Mourning I call;
Our Lord is dead
　That bought us all.

MARY MAGDALENE:

O Jesus Christ, dear Lord of Heaven,
Listen to thy servants' voices!
Whoso believeth not in thee
Shall not be saved, unhappy he!
When his Passion I remember,
My heart is empty, drained of joy,
Alas, that once again I cannot
See thee, Lord, and speak to thee.

MARY, MOTHER OF JAMES:

He is gone to another country,
Accompanied by flights of angels,
And left us here in grief and care.
I pray thee, Lord so gracious,
Send some messenger to us,
That we may have some little knowledge
Of where thou art, and how thou farest.

MARY SALOME:

O Jesus, full of grace and mercy,
Remember us, unhappy women,
Listen to thy servants' voices
When we come into thy kingdom.
So sick I am and faint with longing,
For me there is no further standing.
What shall I do, dear Lord of Heaven?

ALL: (*singing*)

> Alas, mourning I sing,
>> Mourning I call;
> Our Lord is dead
>> That bought us all.

FIRST ANGEL:

> I know whom ye seek:
> But Jesus is not here,
>> For he is risen again,
> Out of the tomb, to life;
> What I speak is true:
>> Christ is risen again.

MARY MAGDALENE:

> O angel, tell me then,
> The body, without peer,
>> Whither is it gone?
> As his grace is great,
> May he grant me with my eyes
>> To see him once again.

SECOND ANGEL:

> Mary, straightway go,
> And Peter and the rest
>> Of his disciples greet;
> For even as he said,
> He will come to Galilee,
>> And there with them will meet.

MARY, MOTHER OF JAMES:

> Then he is risen indeed!
> Jesus our Saviour
>> Is gone from the grave away.
> Glory to him for ever,
> The Lord of earth and heaven,
>> And Prince of sovereignty.

MARY SALOME:

> Let us at once go hence,
> And tell in every place
>> The things that we have seen:
> How the stone is rolled away,
> And from the sepulchre
>> Jesus is risen again.

MARY MAGDALENE:

> Never shall I go hence
> If I do not find my Lord,
>> Who was crucified for men.
> O Jesus, King of grace,
> Grant me to see thee again,
>> Amen, amen!

MARY, MOTHER OF JAMES:

> Mary, mayest thou have
> All the blessings of women,
>> And the blessing of Christ, our Lord.
> From a full heart I pray,
> Grant us now to do good,
>> And always, Almighty God.

MARY MAGDALENE:

> My blessing also on you.
> As thou wentest into the tomb,
>> O Christ, grant us to do good.
> But I pray thee grant me the boon
> Only to see thy face,
>> If so be thy will, O Lord.

MARY SALOME:

> Amen, amen! May we see
> Christ who redeemed us all
>> So painfully with his blood.
> He suffered on the cross
> For love of all the world,
>> As he is almighty God.

Here MARY, *the mother of* JAMES, *and* SALOME, *retire from the tomb.*

MARY MAGDALENE:

As thou didst into the grave descend,
I would that I might meet thee there.
Christ, hear my voice, and hear my prayer,
That thou be with me at the end.

I pray thee, Jesus, grant me grace
And worthiness to meet with thee
Somewhere to-day, that I may see
Once again my beloved's face.

Creator of heaven and earth and sea,
Redeemer ever of us all,
Christ my Saviour, hear my call,
How much I long to speak with thee.

She goes into the garden.

My soul is sick with my desire,
My body broken with my woes;
Is there nobody who knows
Where I may find my Lord and Sire?

She meets JESUS, *supposing him to be the gardener.*

GARDENER (CHRIST):

Woman, whither goest thou,
That so complainest? Weep no more,
For humbly didst thou dry the feet
Of him thou seekest, with thy hair.

MARY MAGDALENE:

Good sir, if thou hast chanced to see
Christ my Lord, where is he now?

If thou canst tell me where he is
Thou shalt have all that I possess.

GARDENER:

Mary! I know that thou hast been
One of his order in this world,
But if thou sawest thy Lord by thee,
Wouldst thou know that it was he?

MARY MAGDALENE:

Yes, yes, indeed, I should know at once
My beloved, Mary's son;
But I see him not in any place,
And so for sorrow I sing 'alas.'

> *And then* JESUS *shall show his side to* MARY
> MAGDALENE, *and he says:*

GARDENER:

Mary, behold my fivefold wounds,
And know in truth I am risen again.
I joy that thou hast grieved for me,
And in my kingdom shalt thou rejoice.

MARY MAGDALENE:

Ah, my beloved, who was dead!
I am unworthy to kiss thy head;
Yet I beseech thee, give me leave
Once again to kiss thy feet.

GARDENER:

Woman, touch me not!
The time will come, but is not yet.
When I have seen my Father's throne
I will return to speak with thee.

MARY MAGDALENE:

Lord, hear my voice, and say the hour
Thou wilt return to speak with us;

Thy disciples are in distress,
And all around is the Jewish power.

GARDENER:

Mary, tell them I will come
As I said, to Galilee,
And thou must bear good cheer from me
To all, and Peter whom much I love.

19

THE ASCENSION

York Tailors' Play

PETER:

O mightful God, how stands it now?
In world thus wild was I not ere.
If he comes—but I know not how
He parts from us when he will fare.
Yet that may for our profit show,
And all his working less and more.
Ah, king of comfort, good art thou,
And true and liking is thy lore.

JOHN:

The missing of my master true,
That dwells not with us lastingly,
Makes me to mourn each day anew,
For wanting of his company.
His peer of goodness ne'er I knew,
Of might nor wisdom equally.

PETER:

That we want him sore may we rue,
For he loved us full faithfully;
And yet in all my misliking
A word that Christ said comforts me.
Our heaviness and our mourning,
He said, to joy should turned be.
That joy, he said in his teaching,
To rob us none of power should be.

Wherefore above all other thing
That joy I long to know and see.

MARY:

Thou Peter, when my son was slain
And laid in grave, you were in care
Whether he should rise, almost each one;
But now you see through knowing clear.
Some things foretold he that are gone
And some to come, but each one sure.
Whether it be to come or none,
We ought to know all will appear.

JESUS:

Almighty God, my Father free,
In earth thy bidding have done,
And glorified the name of thee;
To thyself glorify thy Son.
As thou hast given me authority,
Of all flesh grant me now my boon,
That those thou gavest might living be
In endless life, and all be one.
That life is this that has no end,
To know the Father most of might,
And me the Son whom thou didst send
To die for man without ill plight.
Mankind was thine; thou didst me send,
And took me to thy ruling right;
I died for man, man's miss to mend,
And unto spiteful death was dight.
Thy will unto them taught have I
That would unto my lore incline;
My lore they took obediently;
None of them shall for grief decline.
Thou gravest them me, yet not thereby,
Yet are they thine as well as mine.
Drive them not from our company,
Since they are mine, and mine are thine.
Since they are ours, if they need ought,

Help thou them, if it be thy will;
And as thou knowest I them bought,
For want of help let them not spill.
From the world to take them pray I not,
But that thou keep them aye from ill.
All those so keep who set their thought
In earth my teaching to fulfil.
My tidings take my company
To teach the people where they fare;
In earth shall they live after me,
And suffer sorrows sad and sore;
Despised and hated shall they be,
As I have been, by less and more,
And suffer death in sore degree;
For soothfastness shall none them spare.
Then hallow them, Father, thereby,
In soothfastness so that they may
Be one as we are, you and I,
In will and work both night and day,
And know that I am verily
But soothfastness and life alway;
By which each man of willing way
May win the life that last shall aye.
But ye, my apostles here I mean,
That long have gone about with me,
In great faint-trusting have ye been,
And wondrous hard of hearts are ye.
Worthy to be reproved, I ween,
Are ye forsooth, if ye will see,
In as much as ye all have seen
My work proved and my authority.
When I was dead and laid in grave,
Of my rising ye were in doubt;
And some for my uprising strave
When I was lifelessly laid out
So deep in earth; but since I have
Been walking forty days about,
Eaten with you, your troth to save,
Coming among you in and out.

And therefore be no more in fear
Of mine uprising, day or night;
Your misbelief leave each one here.
For wit ye well, as man of might
Over whom no death shall have power,
I shall be endless life and light.
But for to show you figure clear,
Show I me thuswise to your sight——
How man by course of kind shall rise,
Though he be rotten unto nought,
Out of his grave in this same wise.
At the day of doom shall he be brought
Where I shall sit as true justice
And doom man even as he has wrought.
The wicked to wend with their enemies,
The good to bliss shall they be brought.
Another cause forsooth is this:
On a tree man was betrayed and slain;
I, man, therefore, to mend that miss,
On a tree bought mankind again,
To confusion of him and his
That falsely to forge that fraud was fain,
Mankind to bring again to bliss,
His foe the fiend to endless pain.
The third cause is, truly to tell,
Right as I wend, as well will seem,
So shall I come in flesh and fell
At the day of doom, when I shall deem
The good in endless bliss to dwell,
My foemen from me for to flee,
Without an end in woe to dwell.
Each living man, heed well the same.
But into all the world at hand
The Gospel truly preach shall ye
To every creature alive on land.
Who trusts, if he baptized be,
He shall, if ye shall understand,
Be saved and of all thralldom free;
Who trusts not, as unbelieving found,

For fault of truth condemned is he.
But all these tokens clear and clean
Shall follow them that trust it right——
In my name devils cruel and keen
Shall they cast out of any wight;
With new tongues speak; serpents unclean
Destroy; and if they day or night
Drink venom quick, it shall be seen
To harm them it shall have no might.
On sick folk they their hands shall lay,
And well shall they be soon to wield;
The poor men shall ye have alway,
My company, both in town and field.
And wit ye well, so shall all they
That work my will in youth or eld
Have there a place which I purvey
In bliss with me ever to dwell.
Now is my day's work brought to end,
My time that here to stay was lent.
Up to my Father now I wend
And your Father that down me sent,
My God, your God, and each man's friend
That to his teaching will consent,
To sinners that with sin contend,
That sins amend and will repent.
But since I speak these sayings now
To you, your hearts have heaviness.
Be all fulfilled, profit to show,
That I wend hence, as needful is.
Unless I wend, comes not to you
The comforter of the comfortless;
And if I wend, ye shall find how
I shall send him of my goodness.
My Father's will fulfilled have I,
Therefore farewell, all ye near by.
I go to make a stead ready,
Endless to dwell with me on high.
Send down a cloud, Father, whereby

I come to thee, my Father dear.
My Father's blessing most mighty
Give I to all that I leave here.
Ascendo ad patrem meum.

   Then the angels sing.

MARY:

   Ah, mightful God, aye most of might,
   A wondrous sight is this to see!
   My son thus to be ravished right,
   In a cloud going up from me.
   Both heavy is my heart and light;
   Heavy that such parting should be,
   And light that he holds what he plight,
   And goes thus with authority.
   His promise holds he in each sort;
   That comforts me in all my care.
   But unto whom shall I resort?
   Bewildered so was I never.
   To dwell among these Jews so keen . . .
   Me to despise will they not spare.

JOHN:

   Though he be not in presence seen,
   Yet he is salve of every sore.
   But, lady, since that he betook
   Me for to serve you as your son,
   You need nothing, lady, but look
   What thing in earth you will have done.
   I were to blame if I forsook
   To work your will, mid-day or noon,
   Or any time whereof you spoke.

MARY:

   I thank thee, John, for this thy boon.
   My motherhood, John, shalt thou have,
   And for my son I will thee take.

JOHN:

> That grace, dear lady, would I crave.

MARY:

> My Son's words will I never forsake.
> It were not seeming that we strave
> Nor contraried nought that he spake.
> But, John, till I be brought in grave
> Thou shalt not see my sorrows slake.

JAMES:

> Our worthy Lord, since that he went
> From us, lady, as is his will,
> We thank him that to us has lent
> To live alive here longer still.
> I say for me with full consent,
> Thy liking all will I fulfil.

ANDREW:

> So will we all with great talent;
> Wherefore, lady, give thee not ill.

FIRST ANGEL:

> Ye men of the land of Galilee,
> Why wonder ye, to heaven looking?
> This Jesus, whom from you ye see
> Uptaken, ye shall well understand,
> Right so again come down shall he.
> When he so comes with wounds bleeding,
> Who well has wrought full glad may be,
> Who ill has lived full sore dreading.

SECOND ANGEL:

> Ye that have been his servants true,
> And with him staying night and day,
> Such working as with him ye knew
> Look that ye preach it forth alway.

Your meed in heaven is each day new;
Who serve him, please him well each day.
Who trusts you not, it shall them rue;
They must have pains increasing aye.

JAMES:

Loved be thou, Lord, aye, most of might,
That thus in all our great disease
Comfortest us with thine angels bright.
Now might these Jews their malice cease,
Who saw themselves this wondrous sight
Thus near them wrought under their nose.
And we have matter day and night
Our God more for to praise and please.

ANDREW:

Now may those Jews be all confused,
If they will think on inwardly
How falsely they have him accused,
Unblemished blamed through their envy.
Their falsehood that they long have used,
Now is it proved here openly.
If they upon this matter mused,
It should stir them to ask mercy.

PETER:

That will they not, Andrew; let be;
For they are full of pomp and pride.
It may not avail to thee nor me
Nor none of us with them to chide.
Profit to dwell can I none see,
Wherefore let us no longer bide,
But wend we into each country,
To preach through all this world so wide.

JOHN:

That is our charge, for that is best
That we delay no longer here;
For here get we no place of rest,

To dwell so near the Jewish power.
Us to destroy will they them cast.
Wherefore come forth, my lady dear,
And go we hence. I am full pressed
With you to wend with full good cheer.
My trust is now in every deal
For you to work after your counsel.

JAMES:

My lady dear, that shall you feel
In ought that ever we may avail.
Our comfort is your care to heal;
While we may live you shall not fail.

MARY:

My brethren dear, I trust it well;
My Son shall quit you your travail.

PETER:

To Jerusalem go we again,
And look what after may befall.
Our Lord and master most of main,
He guide you and be with you all.

20

THE LAST JUDGEMENT

York Mercers' Play

GOD:

First when I this world had wrought,
Wood and wind and waters wan
And everything that now is aught,
Full well methought that I did then;
When they were made good I them thought.
Then to my likeness made I man,
And man to grieve me gave he nought.
Thus rue I that I the world began.
When I had made man at my will,
I gave him wits himself to wis;
In Paradise I put him still,
And bade him hold it all as his.
But of the tree of good and ill,
I said "What time thou eatest of this,
Man, thou speedest thyself to spill;
Thou shalt be brought out of all bliss."
But straightway man brake my bidding;
He thought to have been a god thereby;
He thought to have wit of every thing,
In world to have been as wise as I.
He ate the apple I bid should hang;
So he was beguiled through gluttony.
Then both him and his offspring,
To pine I put them all thereby.
Till long and late methought it good
To catch these caitiffs out of care.

I sent my Son with full blithe mood
To earth, to salve them of their sore.
For ruth of them he hung on rood,
And bought them with his body bare;
For them he shed his heart and blood.
What kindness might I do them more?
Then afterward he harried Hell,
And took out those wretches that were therein;
There fought he with those fiends fell
For them that sunken were for sin.
And since in earth he went to dwell,
Examples he gave them, heaven to win;
In Temple himself did teach and tell
To buy them endless bliss therein.
So have they found me full of mercy,
Full of grace and forgiveness,
And they as wretches knowingly
Have led their life in wickedness.
Oft have they grieved me grievously;
Thus they requite me my kindness;
Therefore no longer, certainly,
Will I endure their wickedness.
Men see the world but vanity,
Yet will no man beware thereby;
Each day a mirror may they see,
Yet think they not that they shall die.
All that ever I said should be
Is now fulfilled through prophecy;
Therefore now is it time to me
To make ending of man's folly.
I have endured man many a year
In lust and liking for to spend,
And scarcely find I far or near
A man that will his miss amend.
In earth I see but sinners here;
Therefore mine angels will I send
To blow their trumpets, that all may hear
The time is come when I make end.
Angels, blow your trumpets high,

Every creature for to call;
Learned and lewd, both man and wife,
Receive their doom this day they shall.
Every one that e'er had life,
Be none forgotten, great or small;
There shall they see those wounds five
That my Son suffered for them all.
And sunder them before my sight;
All one in bliss they shall not be.
My blessed children, here on height
On my right hand I shall them see;
And then shall every wicked wight
On my left side for fearing flee.
This day their doom thus have I dight,
To every man as he has served me.

FIRST ANGEL:

Loved be thou, Lord of might the most,
That angels made for messenger.
Thy will shall be fulfilled in haste,
That heaven and earth and hell shall hear.
Good and ill, each single ghost,
Rise, fetch your flesh that ye did bear;
For all this world is brought to waste;
Draw to your doom; nigh comes it near.

SECOND ANGEL:

Every creature both old and young,
Betimes I bid that you arise;
Body and soul now with you bring,
And come before the high justice.
For I am sent from heaven's King,
To call you to his great assise.
Therefore rise up and give reckoning,
How ye served him in every wise.

FIRST GOOD SOUL:

Loved be that Lord who bright does shine,
That in this manner made us rise,

Body and soul together clean,
To come before the high justice.
Let our ill deeds, Lord, be not seen,
That we have wrought in many wise;
But grant us grace and mercy clean,
That we may pass to Paradise.

SECOND GOOD SOUL:

Ah, loved be thou, Lord of all,
That heaven and earth and all hast wrought,
That with thine angels would us call
Out of our graves here to be brought.
Oft have we grieved thee, great and small;
Thereafter, Lord, now doom us not.
Suffer us not to be fiends' thrall,
That oft in earth with sin us sought.

FIRST BAD SOUL:

Alas, alas! That we were born.
So may we sinful caitiffs say.
I hear well by this hideous horn
It draws full near unto Doomsday.
Alas, we wretches are forlorn
That ne'er to please God did essay;
But oft we have his flesh forsworn.
Alas, alas, and welaway!
What shall we wretches do for dread,
Or where for fearing may we flee,
When we may bring forth no good deed
Before him that our Judge shall be?
To ask mercy we have no need,
For well I wot condemned are we.
Alas, that we such life should lead
That drew us to this destiny.
Our wicked works will us destroy,
That we weened never should be witten;
That we did oft full privily,
Openly may we see it written.

Ah, wretches, dear must we abide;
Full smart with hell fire be we smitten;
Now may ne'er soul nor body die,
But with sharp pains evermore be beaten.
Alas, for dread sore may we quake;
Our deeds be our damnation;
For our mismoving must we make;
There is no help in excusation.
We must be set for our sins' sake
For ever far from our salvation,
In hell to dwell with fiends black,
Where never shall there be redemption.

SECOND BAD SOUL:

As careful caitiffs may we rise;
Sore may we wring our hands and weep;
For cursedness and covetise
Damned we be to hell full deep.
Reckoned we never of God's service,
His commandments would we not keep;
But oft times made we sacrifice
To Satan, while others did sleep.
Alas, now wakens all our care;
Our wicked works we may not hide,
But on our backs we must them bear;
They will destroy us on each side.
I see foul fiends to fill our fear,
And all for pomp of wicked pride;
Weep now we may with many a tear.
Alas, that we this day should bide!
Before us plainly shall be brought
The deeds that shall us damn today,
That ears have heard or heart has thought
Since any time that we may say,
That foot has gone or hand has wrought,
That mouth has spoken or eye has seen;
This day full dear shall they be bought.
Alas, unborn that we had been!

THIRD ANGEL:

> Stand not together; part you in two;
> All one shall ye not be in bliss.
> The Father in heaven wills it be so,
> For many of you have wrought amiss.
> Ye good, on his right hand now go;
> The way to heaven shall be this.
> Ye wicked wights, now flee him fro
> On his left hand, as none of his.

GOD (*the Son*):

> This woeful world is brought to an end;
> My Father in heaven wills it to be.
> Therefore to earth now will I wend,
> Myself to sit in majesty.
> To deem my dooms I will descend;
> This body will I bear with me;
> How it was dight, man's sin to mend,
> Now all mankind there shall it see.
> My apostles and my darlings dear,
> The dreadful doom this day is dight.
> Both heaven and earth and hell shall hear
> How I shall hold my promise plight,
> That ye shall sit upon seats here
> Beside myself to see that sight,
> And for to deem folks far and near
> After their working, wrong or right.
> I said also, when I you sent
> To suffer sorrow for my sake,
> All they that would them right repent
> Should with you wend and joyful wake;
> Those to your tales who took no tent
> Should fare to fire with fiends black.
> Of mercy now may nought be meant,
> But as their work was, weal or wrack.
> My promise wholly I fulfil,

Therefore come forth and sit me by,
To hear the doom of good and ill.

A Sixteenth Century note suggests that some lines
have been lost or altered here and six lines later.
"De novo facto," and not copied into this text.

FIRST APOSTLE:

I love thee, Lord God almighty,
Late and early, loud and still;
To do thy bidding fain am I;
I oblige me to do thy will
With all my might, as is worthy.

SECOND APOSTLE:

Ah, mightful God, here is it seen
Thou wilt fulfil thy foreword right,
And all thy sayings will maintain;
I love thee, Lord, with all my might.
Therefore us that have earthly been
Such dignities have dressed and dight.

GOD (*the Son*):

Come forth; I shall sit you between,
And all fulfil that I have plight.

Here he goes to the Judgement seat with the
song of angels.

FIRST DEVIL:

Fellows, array us for to fight;
Our fee to take fast let us go.
The dreadful doom this day is dight;
I dread me that we are full slow.

SECOND DEVIL:

We shall be seen ever in their sight,
And warily wait, else work we wrong;
For if the doomsman do us right,
Full great party shall with us gang.

THIRD DEVIL:

> He shall do right to foe and friend,
> For now shall all the sooth be sought;
> All wicked wights with us shall wend;
> To endless pain shall they be brought.

> > . . . [*A passage (4 lines) "de novo facto" for
> > 1 and 2 Bad Souls lost here.*]

GOD (*the Son*):

> Every creature, take intent
> What bidding now to you I bring.
> This woeful world to nothing went,
> And I am come as crowned king.
> My Father in heaven has me sent
> To deem your deeds and make ending.
> Come is the day of judgment;
> Of sorrow may every sinner sing;
> The day is come of caitiffness,
> All them to grieve that are unclean;
> The day of bale and bitterness;
> Full long abided has it been;
> The day of dread to more and less,
> Of care, of trembling, sorrow keen,
> That every wight that wicked is
> May say "Alas this day is seen!"
> Here may ye see my five wounds wide
> Which I endured for your misdeed,
> Through heart and head, foot, hand and hide,
> Not for my guilt, but for your need.
> Behold my body, back and side,
> How dear I bought your brotherhood.
> These bitter pains would I abide,
> To buy you bliss, thus would I bleed.
> My body was scourged with cruel skill;
> As thief full sorely was I threat;
> On cross they hanged me on a hill
> Bloody and blue as I was beat;

With crown of thorn thrust on full ill,
The spear into my side was set;
My heart blood spared they not to spill;
Man, for thy love I bore it yet.
The Jews spit on me spiteously;
They spared me no more than a thief;
When they struck me I stood full still;
Against them did I nothing grieve.
Behold, mankind, for it is I
That for thee suffered such mischief.
Thus was I dight for thy folly;
See how dear to me was thy life.
Thus was I dight thy sorrow to slake;
Man, thus was I made pledge for thee.
For this did I no vengeance take;
My will it was, for love of thee.
Man, sorely ought you for to quake,
This dreadful day such sight to see.
All this I suffered for thy sake:
Say, man, what suffered thou for me?
My blessed bairns on my right hand,
Your doom this day ye need not dread;
For all your comfort's at command;
Your life in liking shall ye lead.
Come to the kingdom's lasting land
For you prepared for your good deed.
Full blithe may ye be where ye stand,
For mickle in heaven shall be your meed.
When I was hungry, ye me fed,
To slake my thirst your heart was free;
When I was clotheless ye me clad,
Ye would no sorrow on me see.
In hard prison when I was stead,
On my pains then ye had pity;
Full sick when I was brought in bed,
Kindly ye came to comfort me.
When I was weak and weariest,
Ye harboured me full heartily;
Full glad then were ye of your guest,

Supplied my poverty piteously;
At once ye brought me of the best,
And made my bed full easily.
Therefore in heaven shall be your rest,
In joy and bliss to be by me.

FIRST GOOD SOUL:

When had we, Lord that all hast wrought,
Meat or drink wherewith thee to feed,
Since we in earth had never nought
But through the grace of thy godhead?

SECOND GOOD SOUL:

When was't that we clothes to thee brought,
Or visit thee in any need,
Or in thy sickness we thee sought?
Lord, when did we to thee this deed?

GOD (the Son):

My blessed children, hear me say
What time this deed was to me done.
When any that need had, night or day,
Asked for your help and had it soon.
Your free hearts said them never nay,
Early nor late, midday nor noon;
But as ofttimes as they would pray,
They need but bide and have their boon.
Ye cursed caitiffs, kin of Cain,
That ne'er gave comfort in my care,
I and you for ever will be twain,
In dole to dwell for ever more.
Your bitter bales endless begin,
That ye shall have when ye come there;
Ye have deserved so for your sin,
Your grievous deeds that ye did ere.
When I had need of meat and drink,
Caitiffs, ye caught me from your gate;
When ye were set as sirs on bench,

I stood without, weary and wet.
Not one of you would on me think,
Pity to have of my poor state.
Therefore to hell I bid you sink,
And worthy well to go that gate.
When I was sick and sorriest,
Ye visited not, for I was poor;
In prison pent when I was fast,
None of you looked how I might fare.
When I knew never where to rest,
With dints ye drove me from your door;
But ever to pride ye promptly pressed;
My flesh, my blood, oft ye forswore.
Clothesless when I was oft and cold,
For need of you I went all naked;
House nor harbour, help nor hold,
Had I none of you, though I quaked.
My mischief saw ye manifold;
Not one of you my sorrow slaked,
But ever forsook me, young and old.
Therefore shall I now you forsake.

FIRST BAD SOUL:

When hadst thou, Lord that all things has,
Hunger or thirst, since God thou is?
When was it thou in prison was?
When wast thou naked or harbourless?

SECOND BAD SOUL:

When was it we saw thee sick, alas?
When did we this unkindliness,
Weary or wet to let thee pass?
When did we thee this wickedness?

GOD:

Caitiffs, as oft as did betide
The needful asked ought in my name,
Ye heard them not, your ears ye hid,
Your help to them was not at home—

To me ye that unkindness did;
Therefore ye bear this bitter blame.
To least or most when ye it did,
To me ye did the self and same.
My chosen children, come to me;
With me to dwell now shall ye wend.
There joy and bliss shall ever be;
Your life in liking shall ye spend.
Ye cursed caitiffs, from me flee,
In hell to dwell without an end.
There shall ye nought but sorrow see,
And dwell by Satanas the fiend.
Now is fulfilled all my forethought,
For ended is each earthly thing.
All wights in earth that I have wrought
After their works have now winning;
They that would sin and ceased not,
Of sorrows sore now shall they sing;
And they that mended while they might
Shall dwell and bide in my blessing.

*And so he makes an end with a melody of angels
passing from place to place.*

Handwritten annotations at top of page:

1. Fellowship — forsakes Everyman
2. Kindred
3. Goods (riches) desert him as are only lent **21**
4. Good Deeds is too weak to go with him
5. Knowledge take Everyman to confession who gives him scourge of repentence.
6. Strength, Discretion, Five Wits and Beauty go with Everyman
7. all forsake him except Good Deeds + Knowledge

EVERYMAN

Here beginneth a treatise how ye high Father of Heaven
sendeth Death to summon every creature to come and give
account of their lives in this world, and is in manner of a
Moral play.

Enter MESSENGER.

MESSENGER:

I pray you all give your audience,
And hear this matter with reverence,
By figure a moral play.
The Summoning of Everyman called it is,
That of our lives and ending shews
How transitory we be all day.
This matter is wondrous precious;
But the intent of it is more gracious
And sweet to bear away.
The story saith:—Man, in the beginning
Look well, and take good heed to the ending,
Be you never so gay!
Ye think sin in the beginning full sweet,
Which in the end causeth thy soul to weep
When the body lyeth in clay.
Here shall you see how *Fellowship* and *Jollity,*
Both *Strength, Pleasure,* and *Beauty,*
Will fade from thee as flower in May;
For ye shall hear how our heaven king
Calleth *Everyman* to a general reckoning.
Give audience, and hear what he doth say.

The MESSENGER *goes and* GOD *enters.*

GOD:

I perceive, here in my Majesty,
How that all creatures be to me unkind,
Living without dread in worldly prosperity.
Of ghostly sight the people be so blind,
Drowned in sin, they know me not for their God.
In wordly riches is all their mind.
They fear not my rightwiseness, the sharp rod;
My love that I showed when I for them died
They forget clean, and shedding of my blood red.
I hanged between two thieves, it cannot be denied;
To get them life I suffered to be dead;
I healed their feet, with thorns hurt was my head;
I could do no more than I did, truly;
And now I see the people do clean forsake me.
They use the seven deadly sins damnable.
As pride, covetous, wrath, and lechery
Now in the world be made commendable,
And thus they leave of angels ye heavenly company.
Every man liveth so after his own pleasure,
And yet of their life they be nothing sure.
I see the more that I them forbear
The worse they be from year to year.
All that liveth impaireth fast.
Therefore I will, in all the haste,
Have a reckoning of every man's person;
For and I leave the people thus alone
In their life and wicked tempests,
Verily they will become much worse than beasts.
For now one would by envy another up eat;
Charity they do all clean forget.
I hoped well that every man
In my glory should make his mansion;
And thereto I had them all elect.
But now I see like traitors deject
They thank me not for ye pleasure that I to them meant,
Nor yet for their being that I them have lent.
I preferred the people great multitude of mercy,

And few there be that asketh it heartily.
They be so cumbered with worldly riches
That needs on them I must do justice,
On every man living, without fear.
Where art thou, *Death*, thou mighty messenger?

> DEATH *enters from the entrance to the Grave.*

DEATH:
Almighty God I am here at your will,
Your commandment to fulfill.

GOD:
Go thou to *Everyman*
And shew him, in my name,
A pilgrimage he must on him take,
Which he in no wise may escape;
And that he bring with him a sure reckoning
Without delay or any tarrying.

DEATH:
Lord, I will in the world go run over all,
And cruelly outsearch both great and small.
Every man will I beset that liveth beastly
Out of God's laws and dreadeth not folly.
He that loveth riches I will strike with my dart,
His sight to blind, and from Heaven to depart—
Except that alms be his good friend—
In Hell for to dwell, world without end.

> *Exit* GOD. DEATH *moves to stage of the World.*

Lo, yonder I see *Everyman* walking.
Full little he thinketh on my coming;
His mind is on fleshly lusts, and his treasure;
And great pain it shall cause him to endure
Before the Lord, Heaven's king.

> EVERYMAN *enters with a company of men and women.*
> *They break into a dance.* DEATH *watches awhile.*

Everyman, stand still! Whither art thou going
Thus gaily? Hast thou thy Maker forgot?

EVERYMAN: (*still dancing*)
Why askest thou?
Wouldest thou wit?*

DEATH:
Yea, sir; I will shew you:
In great haste I am sent to thee
From God out of his Majesty.

EVERYMAN: (*faltering*)
What, sent to me?

DEATH:
Yea, certainly.
Though thou have forgot him here,
He thinketh on thee in the heavenly sphere,
As, or we depart, thou shalt know.

EVERYMAN:
What desireth God of me?

DEATH:
That shall I shew thee.
A reckoning he will needs have
Without any longer respite.

EVERYMAN:
To give a reckoning longer leisure I crave.
This blind matter troubleth my wit.

DEATH:
On thee thou must take a long journey.
Therefore thy book of count with thee thou bring,
For turn again thou cannot by no way!
And look thou be sure of thy reckoning
For before God thou shalt answer and shew
Thy many bad deeds and good but a few,

* 'Wit' and 'wete'—both derive from a Saxon verb meaning
'to know.'

How thou hast spent thy life, and in what wise,
Before the chief Lord of Paradise.
Have a do that we were in that way,
For wete thou well thou shalt make none thy attornay.

EVERYMAN:

Full unready I am such reckoning to give.
I know thee not. What messenger art thou?

DEATH:

I am *Death* that no man dreadeth.
Every man I arrest and no man spareth;
For it is God's commandment
That all to me should be obedient.

The dance peters out and the guests leave.

[handwritten note: Unready— Tries to bribe Death]

EVERYMAN:

O *Death*, thou comest when I had ye least in mind!
In thy power it lyeth me to save;
Yet of my goods will I give ye, if thou will be kind;
Yea, a thousand pound shalt thou have
And thou defer this matter till another day.

DEATH:

Everyman, it may not be, by no way!
I set not by gold, silver, nor riches,
Ne by Pope, Emperor, King, Duke, ne princes;
For and I would receive gifts great,
All the world I might get.
But my custom is clean contrary.
I give thee no respite. Come hence, and not tarry!

EVERYMAN:

Alas, shall I have no longer respite?
I may say *Death* giveth no warning!
To think on thee it maketh my heart sick,
For all unready is my book of reckoning.
But twelve year and I might have abiding,
My counting book I would make so clear

That my reckoning I should not need to fear.
Wherefore, *Death*, I pray thee, for God's mercy,
Spare me till I be provided of remedy!

DEATH:

Thee availeth not to cry, weep, and pray,
But haste thee lightly that thou wert gone that journey!
And prove thy friends, if thou can.
For wete thou well the tide abideth no man;
And in the world each living creature
For Adam's sin must die of nature.

EVERYMAN:

Death, if I should this pilgrimage take,
And my reckoning surely make,
Shew me for Saint Charity,
Should I not come again shortly?

DEATH:

No, *Everyman;* and thou be once there,
Thou may'st never more come here,
Trust me verily.

EVERYMAN:

O gracious God in the high seat celestial,
Have mercy on me in this most need!
Shall I have no company from this vale terrestrial
Of my acquaintance that way me to lead?

DEATH:

Yea, if any be so hardy
That would go with thee and bear thee company.
Hie thee that thou wert gone to God's magnificence,
Thy reckoning to give before his presence.
What, weenest thou thy life is given thee
And thy worldly goods also?

EVERYMAN:
I had weened so, verily.

DEATH:
Nay, nay, they were but lent thee;
For as soon as thou art gone
Another awhile shall have it, and then go therefrom
Even as thou hast done.
Everyman, thou art mad! Thou hast thy wits five
And here on earth will not amend thy life;
For suddenly I do come.

EVERYMAN:
O wretched caitiff, whither shall I flee
That I might 'scape this endless sorrow!
Now, gentle *Death,* spare me till tomorrow,
That I may amend me
With good advisement.

DEATH:
Nay, thereto I will not consent,
Nor no man will I respite;
But to the heart suddenly I shall smite
Without any advisement.
And now out of thy sight I will me hie.
See thou make thee ready shortly
For thou mayest say this is the day
That no man living may scape away.

DEATH *goes.*

EVERYMAN:
Alas, I may well weep with sighs deep!
Now have I no manner of company
To help me in my journey and me to keep;
And also my writing is full unready.
How shall I do now for to excuse me?
I would to God I had never been got!

To my soul a full great profit it had been,
For now I fear pains huge and great.

> *A distant clock strikes.*

The time passeth. Lord, help, that all wrought!
For though I mourn it availeth nought;
The day passeth and is almost agone.
I wot not well what for to do.
To whom were I best my complaint to make?
What and I to *Fellowship* thereof spake,
And shewed him of this sudden chance?
For in him is all mine affiance.
We have in the world so many a day
Been good friends in sport and play.
I see him yonder certainly.
I trust that he will bear me company,
Therefore to him will I speak to ease my sorrow.
Well met, good *Fellowship!* and good morrow!

> FELLOWSHIP *has entered in the meantime.*

FELLOWSHIP:
Everyman, good morrow, by this day!
Sir, why lookest thou so piteously?
If anything be amiss, I pray thee me say,
That I may help to remedy.

EVERYMAN:
Yea, good *Fellowship,* yea,
I am in great jeopardy.

FELLOWSHIP:
My true friend, show to me your mind;
I will not forsake thee to my life's end
In the way of good company.

EVERYMAN:
That was well spoken and lovingly.

FELLOWSHIP:

Sir, I must needs know your heaviness;
I have pity to see you in any distress.
If any have you wronged, ye shall revenged be,
Though I on the ground be slain for thee,
Though that I know before that I should die.

EVERYMAN:

Verily, *Fellowship*, gramercy.

FELLOWSHIP:

Tush, by thy thanks I set not a straw!
Shew me your grief and say no more.

EVERYMAN:

If I my heart should to you break
And then you to turn your mind from me
And would not me comfort when ye hear me speak,
Then should I ten times sorrier be.

FELLOWSHIP:

Sir, I say as I will do indeed.

EVERYMAN:

Then be you a good friend at need.
I have found you true here before.

FELLOWSHIP:

And so ye shall evermore;
For, in faith, and thou go to hell
I will not forsake thee by the way.

EVERYMAN:

Ye speak like a good friend. I believe you well.
I shall deserve it and I may.

FELLOWSHIP:

I speak of no deserving, by this day!
For he that will say and nothing do

Is not worthy with good company to go.
Therefore show me the grief of your mind,
As to your friend most loving and kind.

EVERYMAN:
I shall shew you how it is.
Commanded I am to go a journey—
A long way, hard and dangerous—
And give a straight count, without delay,
Before the high judge, Adonay.
Wherefore I pray you, bear me company,
As ye have promised, in this journay.

FELLOWSHIP:
This is matter indeed! Promise is duty.
But and I should take such a voyage on me,
I know it well it should be to my pain.
Also it make me afeard, certain.
But let us take counsel here, as well as we can,
For your words would fear a strong man.

EVERYMAN:
Why ye said if I had need
Ye would me never forsake, quick nor dead,
Though it were to hell truly.

FELLOWSHIP:
So I said certainly.
But such pleasures be set aside, the sooth to say.
And also if we took such a journay,
When should we come again?

EVERYMAN:
Nay never again till the day of doom!

FELLOWSHIP:
In faith, then will I not come there!
Who hath you these tidings brought?

EVERYMAN:
Indeed, *Death* was with me here.

FELLOWSHIP: (*backing away in fear*)
Now, by God, that all hath bought,
If *Death* were the messenger,
For no man that is living today
I will not go that loath journay—
Not for the father that begat me!

EVERYMAN:
Ye promised otherwise, pardee.

FELLOWSHIP:
I wot well I said so, truly.
And yet if thou wilt eat and drink and make good cheer,
Or haunt to women the lusty company,
I would not forsake you while the day is clear,
Trust me, verily.

EVERYMAN:
Yea, thereto ye would be ready!
To go to mirth, solace, and play
Your mind will sooner apply,
Than to bear me company in my long journay.

FELLOWSHIP:
Nay in good faith I will not that way.
But an thou wilt murder, or any man kill,
In that I will help thee with a good will.

EVERYMAN:
O that is a simple advice indeed.
Gentle *Fellow*, help me in my necessity!
We have loved long and now I need;
And now, gentle *Fellowship*, remember me.

FELLOWSHIP:

Whether ye have loved me or no,
By Saint John I will not with thee go!

EVERYMAN:

Yet, I pray thee, take ye labour and do so much for me
To bring me forward, for Saint Charity,
And comfort me till I come without the town.

FELLOWSHIP:

Nay, and thou would give me a new gown
I will not a foot with thee go.
But an thou had tarried I would not have left thee so.
And as now God speed thee in thy journay!
For from thee I will depart as fast as I may.

EVERYMAN:

Whither away, *Fellowship?* Will ye forsake me?

FELLOWSHIP:

Yea, by my faith! To God I betake thee.

EVERYMAN:

Farewell, good *Fellowship!* For ye my heart is sore.
Adieu for ever. I shall see thee no more.

FELLOWSHIP:

In faith, *Everyman,* fare well now at the end!
For you I will remember that parting is mourning.

    FELLOWSHIP *hurries away.*

EVERYMAN:

Alack! Shall we thus depart indeed—
Ah, Lady, help!—without any more comfort?
Lo, *Fellowship* forsaketh me in my most need.
For help in this world whither shall I resort?
Fellowship here before with me would merry make,

And now little sorrow for me doth he take.
It is said, "In prosperity men friends may find
Which in adversity be full unkind."
Now whither for succour shall I flee,
Sith that *Fellowship* hath forsaken me?
To my kinsmen I will, truly,
Praying them to help me in my necessity.
I believe that they will do so,
For "kind will creep where it may not go."
I will go assay, for yonder I see them go.
Where be ye now, my friends and kinsmen?

Enter KINDRED, COUSIN, *and her* MAID.

KINDRED: (*making a reverence*)
Here be we now at your commandment.
Cousin, I pray you show us your intent
In any wise and do not spare.

COUSIN:
Yea, *Everyman,* and to us declare
If ye be disposed to go any whither;
For wete you well we will live and die together.

KINDRED:
In wealth and woe we will with you hold,
For over his kin a man may be bold.

EVERYMAN:
Gramercy, my friends and kinsmen kind.
Now shall I show you the grief of my mind.
I was commanded by a messenger
That is a high king's chief officer.
He bad me go a pilgrimage to my pain,
And I know well I shall never come again.
Also I must give a reckoning straight,
For I have a great enemy that for me doth wait,
Which intendeth me for to hinder.

KINDRED: (*alarmed*)
What account is that which ye must render?
That would I know.

EVERYMAN:
Of all my works I must show
How I have lived and my days spent;
Also of ill deeds that I have used
In my time sith life was me lent,
And of all virtues that I have refused.
Therefore I pray you go thither with me
To help to make mine account, for Saint Charity.

COUSIN:
What? To go thither? Is that the matter?
Nay, *Everyman,* I had liefer fast bread and water
All this five year and more.

EVERYMAN:
Alas that ever I was born!
For now shall I never be merry
If that you forsake me.

KINDRED:
Ah, sir, what? Ye be a merry man!
Take good heart to you and make no moan.
But one thing I warn you, by Saint Anne—
As for me ye shall go alone.

EVERYMAN:
My *Cousin,* will you not with me go?

COUSIN:
No, by Our Lady! I have the cramp in my toe.
Trust not to me; for, so God me speed,
I will deceive you in your most need.

KINDRED:

It availeth not us to tyse.*
Ye shall have my maid with all my heart;
She loveth to go to feasts, there to be nice,
And to dance, and abroad to start.
I will give her leave to help you in that journay,
If that you and she may agree.

EVERYMAN:

Now show me the very effect of your mind;
Will you go with me or abide behind?

KINDRED:

Abide behind? yea, that will I and I may!
Therefore farewell till another day!

    KINDRED *goes.*

EVERYMAN:

How should I be merry or glad?
For fair promises men to me make,
But when I have most need they me forsake.
I am deceived: that maketh me sad.

COUSIN:

Cousin *Everyman,* farewell now;
For verily I will not go with you.
Also of mine own life an unready reckoning
I have to account; therefore I make tarrying.
Now God keep thee, for now I go.

    COUSIN *goes, followed by the* MAID.

EVERYMAN:

Ah, Jesus, is all come hereto?
Lo, fair words maketh fools fayne;
They promise, and nothing will do certain.
My kinsmen promised me faithfully

* Bargain.

For to abide with me steadfastly,
And now fast away do they flee.
Even so *Fellowship* promised me.
What friend were best me of to provide?
I lose my time here longer to abide;
Yet in my mind a thing there is:
All my life I have loved riches;
If that my *Goods* now help me might
He would make my heart full light.
I will speak to him in this distress.
Where art thou, my *Goods* and riches?

GOODS: (*within*)
Who calleth me? *Everyman?* What, hast thou haste?
I lie here in corners, trussed and piled so high
And in chests I am locked so fast,
Also sacked in bags—thou mayest see with thine eye—
I can not stir. In packs, low I lie.
What would ye have? lightly me say.

EVERYMAN:
Come hither, *Goods,* in all the haste thou may,
For of counsel I must desire thee.

GOODS *enters.*

GOODS:
Sir, and ye in the world have sorrow or adversity,
That can I help you to remedy shortly.

EVERYMAN:
It is another disease that grieveth me;
In this world it is not, I tell thee so.
I am sent for an other way to go,
To give a straight account general
Before the highest Jupiter of all.
And all my life I have had joy and pleasure in thee,
Therefore, I pray thee, go with me.
For, peradventure, thou mayest before God Almighty

My reckoning help to clean and purify.
For it is said ever among
That "money maketh all right that is wrong."

GOODS:

Nay, *Everyman*, I sing another song.
I follow no man in such voyages;
For and I went with thee
Thou shouldest fare much the worse for me;
For because on me thou did set thy mind
Thy reckoning I have made blotted and blind,
That thine account thou can not make truly—
And that hast thou for the love of me!

EVERYMAN:

That would grieve me full sore
When I should come to that fearful answer.
Up! Let us go thither together!

GOODS:

Nay, not so! I am too brittle: I may not endure.
I will follow no man one foot, be ye sure.

EVERYMAN:

Alas, I have thee loved, and had great pleasure
All my life-days on goods and treasure.

GOODS:

That is to thy damnation, without lying!
For my love is contrary to the love everlasting.
But if thou had me loved moderately during,
As to the poor to give part of me,
Then shouldest thou not in this dolour be,
Nor in this great sorrow and care.

EVERYMAN:

Lo, now was I deceived or I was ware;
And all I may wete my spending of time.

GOODS:
What, weenest thou that I am thine?

EVERYMAN:
I had weened so.

GOODS:
Nay, *Everyman,* I say no.
As for a while I was lent thee,
A season thou hast had me in prosperity.
My condition is man's soul to kill;
If I save one, a thousand I do spill.
Weenest thou that I will follow thee
From this world? Nay, verily.

EVERYMAN:
I had weened otherwise.

GOODS:
Therefore to thy soul *Goods* is a thief,
For when thou art dead, this is my guise—
Another to deceive in this same wise
As I have done thee, and all to his soul's reprief.

EVERYMAN:
O false *Goods,* cursed may thou be,
Thou traitor to God that hast deceived me
And caught me in thy snare!

GOODS:
Marry, thou brought thyself in care,
Whereof I am right glad.
I must needs laugh; I cannot be sad.

EVERYMAN:
Ah, *Goods,* thou hast had long my heartily love:
I gave thee that which should be the Lord's above.
But wilt thou not go with me indeed?
I pray thee truth to say.

GOODS:

No, so God me speed!
Therefore, farewell, and have good day!

GOODS *goes.*

EVERYMAN:

O to whom shall I make my moan
For to go with me in that heavy journay?
First *Fellowship* said he would with me gone—
His words were very pleasant and gay—
But afterward he left me alone.
Then spake I to my kinsmen all in despair,
And also they gave me words fair—
They lacked no fair speaking!
But all forsake me in the ending!
Then went I to my *Goods* that I loved best
In hope to have comfort; but there had I least,
For my *Goods* sharply did me tell
That he bringeth many into hell.
Then of myself I was ashamed,
And so I am worthy to be blamed.
Thus may I well myself hate.
Of whom shall I now counsel take?
I think that I shall never speed
Till that I go to my *Good Deed.*
But alas, she is so weak
That she can neither go nor speak.
Yet will I venture on her now.
My *Good Deeds*, where be you?

GOOD DEEDS *is discovered on the middle stage.*

GOOD DEEDS:

Here I lie, cold in the ground.
Thy sins hath me sore bound,
That I can not stir.

EVERYMAN:
O *Good Deeds,* I stand in fear!
I must you pray of counsel,
For help now should come right well.

GOOD DEEDS:
Everyman, I have understanding
That ye be summoned account to make
Before Messias of Jerusalem King,
And you do by me, that journey with you will I take.

EVERYMAN:
Therefore I come to you my moan to make.
I pray you that ye will go with me.

GOOD DEEDS:
I would full fain, but I cannot stand, verily.

EVERYMAN:
Why, is there anything on you fall?

GOOD DEEDS:
Yea, sir, I may thank you of all.
If you had perfectly cheered me
Your book of count full ready had been.

GOOD DEEDS *shows* EVERYMAN *the book.*

Look, the books of your works and deeds also.
Behold, how they lie under the feet,
To your soul's heaviness!

EVERYMAN:
Our Lord Jesus help me!
For one letter here I can not see.

GOOD DEEDS:
There is a blind reckoning in time of distress.

EVERYMAN:
Good Deeds, I pray you help me in this need
Or else I am for ever damned indeed!
Therefore help me to make my reckoning
Before the Redeemer of all thing,
That King is, and was, and ever shall.

GOOD DEEDS:
Everyman, I am sorry of your fall
And fain would I help you and I were able.

EVERYMAN:
Good Deeds, your counsel I pray you give me.

GOOD DEEDS:
That shall I do verily.
Though that on my feet I may not go,
I have a sister that shall with you also
Called *Knowledge*, which shall with you abide
To help you to make that dreadful reckoning.

> KNOWLEDGE *enters.*

KNOWLEDGE:
Everyman, I will go with thee and be thy guide
In thy most need to go by thy side.

EVERYMAN:
In good condition I am now in every thing
And am whole content with this good thing,
Thanked be God, my creator!

GOOD DEEDS:
And when he hath brought you there
Where thou shalt heal thee of thy smart,
Then go you with your reckoning and your *Good Deeds*
together
For to make you joyful at heart
Before the Blessed Trinity.

EVERYMAN:

My *Good Deeds*, gramercy!
I am well content, certainly,
With your words sweet.

KNOWLEDGE: (*moving to the stage of the world*)
Now go we together lovingly
To *Confession*, that cleansing river.

EVERYMAN:

For joy I weep! I would we were there
But, I pray you, give me cognition
Where dwelleth that holy man, *Confession?*

KNOWLEDGE:

In the House of Salvation.
We shall find him in that place
That shall us comfort, by God's grace.

> EVERYMAN *follows* KNOWLEDGE *to the Confessional
> and kneels.* CONFESSION *enters.*

Lo, this is *Confession*. Kneel down and ask mercy,
For he is in good conceit with God Almighty.

EVERYMAN:

O glorious fountain, that all uncleanness doth clarify,
Wash from me the spots of vice unclean,
That on me no sin may be seen!
I come, with *Knowledge*, for my redemption,
Redempt with heart and full contrition;
For I am commanded a pilgrimage to take,
And great accounts before God to make.
Now I pray you, *Shrift*, mother of salvation,
Help my *Good Deeds* for my piteous exclamation.

CONFESSION:

I know your sorrow well, *Everyman*.
Because with *Knowledge* ye come to me

I will you comfort as well as I can;
And a precious jewel I will give thee
Called penance, voyder* of adversity.
Therewith shall your body chastised be
With abstinence, and perseverance in God's service.
Here shall you receive that scourge of me
Which is penance strong that ye must endure
To remember thy Saviour was scourged for thee
With sharp scourges, and suffered it patiently.
So must thou, or thou scape that painful pilgrimage.

CONFESSION *gives the scourge to* KNOWLEDGE.

Knowledge, keep him in this voyage,
And by that time *Good Deeds* will be with thee.
But in any wise be sure of mercy,
For your time draweth fast; and ye will saved be
Ask God mercy and he will grant truly.
When with the scourge of penance man doth him bind,
The oil of forgiveness then shall he find.

EVERYMAN:
Thanked be God for his gracious work!
For now I will my penance begin.
This hath rejoiced and lighted my heart,
Though the knots be painful and hard within.

KNOWLEDGE:
Everyman, look your penance that ye fulfill,
What pain that ever it to you be;
And *Knowledge* shall give you counsel at will
How your account ye shall make clearly.

EVERYMAN *kneels in prayer.*

EVERYMAN:
O eternal God! O heavenly figure!
O way of rightwiseness! O goodly vision,

* Screen or defence.

Which descended down in a virgin pure
Because he would every man redeem,
Which Adam forfeited by his disobedience!
O blessed Godhead elect and high divine,
Forgive me my grievous offence!
Here I cry thee mercy in this presence.
O ghostly treasure! O merciful redeemer!
Of all the world hope and conductor!
Mirror of joy and founder of mercy!
Which illumineth Heaven and earth thereby,
Hear my clamorous complaint though it late be.
Receive my prayers unworthy in this heavy life
Though I be a sinner most abominable
Yet let my name be written in Moses table.
O Mary, pray to the Maker of all thing
Me for to help at my ending,
And save me from the power of my enemy;
For *Death* assaileth me strongly.
And Lady, that I may by means of thy prayer
Of your Son's glory to be partaker
By the means of his passion I it crave
I beseech you help me my soul to save.

> *He rises.*

Knowledge, give me the scourge of penance.
My flesh therewith shall give a quittance.
I will now begin if God give me grace.

KNOWLEDGE:
Everyman, God give you time and space!
Thus I bequeath you in ye hands of our Saviour.
Now may you make your reckoning sure.

EVERYMAN:
In the name of the Holy Trinity
My body sore punished shall be.

> EVERYMAN *scourges himself during the following speech.*

Take this, body, for the sin of the flesh!
Also thou delightest to go gay and fresh
And in the way of damnation thou did me bring.
Therefore suffer now strokes of punishing.
Now of penance I will wade the water clear
To save me from Purgatory, that sharp fire.

GOOD DEEDS: (*rising*)
I thank God, now I can walk and go
And am delivered of my sickness and woe.
Therefore with *Everyman* I will go, and not spare.
His good works I will help him to declare.

KNOWLEDGE:
Now *Everyman*, be merry and glad!
Your *Good Deeds* cometh now, ye may not be sad.
Now is your *Good Deeds* whole and sound,
Going upright upon the ground.

EVERYMAN:
My heart is light and shall be evermore.
Now will I smite faster than I did before.

GOOD DEEDS:
Everyman, pilgrim, my special friend,
Blessed be thou without end!
For thee is preparate the eternal glory.
Ye have me made whole and sound,
Therefore I will bide by thee in every stound.*

EVERYMAN:
Welcome, my *Good Deeds*! Now I hear thy voice
I weep for very sweetness of love.

KNOWLEDGE:
Be no more sad, but ever rejoice;
God seeth thy living on his throne above;

* Sorrow.

Put on this garment to thy behove
Which is wet with your tears
Or else before God you may it miss
When ye to your journey's end come shall.

EVERYMAN:

Gentle *Knowledge*, what do you it call?

KNOWLEDGE:

It is a garment of sorrow;
From pain it will you borrow;
Contrition it is
That getteth forgiveness,
It pleaseth God passing well.

GOOD DEEDS:

Everyman, will you wear it for your health?

EVERYMAN *puts on the garment of contrition.*

EVERYMAN:

Now blessed be Jesu, Mary's son,
For now have I on true contrition.
And let us go now without tarrying.
Good Deeds, have we clear our reckoning?

EVERYMAN, GOOD DEEDS *and* KNOWLEDGE *move to the middle stage.*

GOOD DEEDS:

Yea, indeed, I have it here.

EVERYMAN:

Then I trust we need not fear.
Now friends, let us not part in twain.

KNOWLEDGE:

Nay, *Everyman*, that will we not, certain.

GOOD DEEDS:
Yet must thou lead with thee
Three persons of great might.

EVERYMAN:
Who should they be?

GOOD DEEDS:
Discretion and *Strength* they hight,
And thy *Beauty* may not abide behind.

KNOWLEDGE:
Also we must call to mind
Your *Five Wits* as for your counsellors.

GOOD DEEDS:
You must have them ready at all hours.

EVERYMAN:
How shall I get them hither?

KNOWLEDGE:
You must call them all together,
And they will hear you incontinent.*

EVERYMAN:
My friends, come hither and be present,
Discretion, Strength, my *Five Wits,* and *Beauty!*

> *Enter gaily* DISCRETION, STRENGTH, FIVE WITS, *and*
> BEAUTY.

BEAUTY:
Here at your will we be all ready.
What will ye that we should do?

GOOD DEEDS:
That ye would with *Everyman* go

* Immediately.

And help him in his pilgimage.
Advise you: will ye with him or not in that voyage?

STRENGTH:

We will bring him all thither
To his help and comfort, ye may believe me.

DISCRETION:

So will we go with him altogether.

EVERYMAN:

Almighty God, loved may thou be!
I give thee laud that I have hither brought
Strength, Discretion, Beauty, and *Five Wits.* Lack I
  nought.
And my *Good Deeds* with *Knowledge* clear
All be in company at my will here.
I desire no more to my business.

STRENGTH:

And I, *Strength,* will by you stand in distress,
Though thou would in battle fight on the ground.

FIVE WITS:

And though it were through the world round
We will not depart for sweet nor sour.

BEAUTY:

No more will I, unto death's hour,
Whatsoever thereof befall.

DISCRETION:

Everyman, advise you first of all;
Go with a good advisement and deliberation.
We all give you virtuous monition
That all shall be well.

EVERYMAN:

My friends, hearken what I will tell—
I pray God reward you in his heavenly sphere—

Now hearken all that be here,
For I will make my testament
Here before you all present:
In alms half my goods I will give with my hands twain
In the way of charity with good intent,
And the other half still shall remain,
I it bequeath to be returned there it ought to be.
This I do in despite of the fiend of hell
To go quite out of his peril
Ever after and this day.

KNOWLEDGE:

Everyman, hearken what I say:
Go to priesthood, I you advise,
And receive of him, in any wise,
The holy sacrament and ointment together;
Then shortly see ye turn again hither:
We will all abide you here.

FIVE WITS:

Yea, *Everyman*, hie you that ye ready were.
There is no Emperor, King, Duke, nor Baron
That of God hath commission
As hath the least priest in the world being;
For of the blessed sacraments pure and benign
He beareth the keys, and thereof hath the cure
For man's redemption—it is ever sure—
Which God for our soul's medicine
Gave us out of his heart with great pain,
Here in this transitory life for thee and me.
The blessed sacraments seven there be—
Baptism, confirmation, with priesthood good,
And ye sacrament of God's precious flesh and blood,
Marriage, the holy extreme unction, and penance.
These seven be good to have in remembrance,
Gracious sacraments of high divinity.

EVERYMAN:

Fain would I receive that holy body,
And meekly to my ghostly father I will go.

FIVE WITS:

Everyman, that is the best that ye can do.
God will you to salvation bring.

> EVERYMAN *goes out to receive the sacrament from the priest. The others remain.*

For priesthood exceedeth all other thing:
To us holy scripture they do teach,
And converteth man from sin, heaven to reach;
God hath to them more power given
Than to any angel that is in heaven.
With five words he may consecrate
God's body in flesh and blood to make,
And handleth his Maker between his hands.
The priest bindeth and unbindeth all bands,
But in earth and in heaven.
Thou ministers all the sacraments seven;
Though we kissed thy feet, thou wert worthy;
Thou art the surgeon that cureth sin deadly
No remedy we find under God
But all only priesthood.
God gave priests that dignity
And setteth them in his stead among us to be.
Thus they be above angels in degree.

KNOWLEDGE:

If priests be good, it is so surely.
But when Jesu hanged on ye cross with great smart,
There he gave out of his blessed heart
The same sacrament in great torment.
He sold them not to us, that Lord omnipotent;
Therefore Saint Peter the Apostle doth say
That Jesus curse hath all they
Which God their Saviour do buy or sell,
Or they for any money do take or tell.
Sinful priests giveth the sinners example bad:
There children sitteth by other men's fires, I have heard;
And some haunteth woman's company

With unclean life, as lusts of lechery.
These be with sin made blind.

FIVE WITS:

I trust to God no such may we find.
Therefore let us priesthood honour,
And follow their doctrine for our soul's succour.
We be their sheep and they shepherds be,
By whom we all be kept in surety.
Peace! For yonder I see *Everyman* come,
Which hath made true satisfaction.

GOOD DEEDS:

Methinketh it is he indeed.

  EVERYMAN *returns bearing a rood.*

EVERYMAN:

Now Jesu be our alder* speed.
I have received the sacrament for my redemption,
And then mine extreme unction.
Blessed be all they that counselled me to take it!
And now, friends, let us go without longer respite.
I thank God that ye have tarried so long.
Now set each of you on this rood your hand
And shortly follow me.
I go before there I would be. God be our guide!

STRENGTH:

Everyman, we will not from you go
Till ye have done this voyage long.

DISCRETION:

I, *Discretion,* will bide by you also.

KNOWLEDGE:

And though this pilgrimage be never so strong,
I will never part you from.

  * Of all.

STRENGTH:

Everyman, I will be as sure by thee
As ever I did by Judas Maccabee.

> *They proceed together in pilgrimage to the Stage of
> the Grave, singing. At the mouth of the grave,* DEATH
> *is awaiting* EVERYMAN.

EVERYMAN:

Alas, I am so faint I may not stand.
My limbs under me do fold.
Friends, let us not turn again to this land,
Not for all the world's gold;
For into this cave must I creep
And turn to earth, and there to sleep.

BEAUTY:

What, into this grave? Alas!

EVERYMAN:

Yea, there shall ye consume, the more and less.

BEAUTY:

And what, should I smother here?

EVERYMAN:

Yea, by my faith and never more appear.
In this world live no more we shall,
But in Heaven before the highest Lord of all.

BEAUTY:

I cross out all this! Adieu, by Saint John!
I take my cap in my lap and am gone.

EVERYMAN:

What, *Beauty*, whither will ye?

BEAUTY:

Peace! I am deaf. I look not behind me,
Not an thou wouldest give me all ye gold in thy chest.

BEAUTY *goes.*

EVERYMAN:

Alas, whereto may I trust?
Beauty goeth fast away from me.
She promised with me to live and die.

STRENGTH:

Everyman, I will thee also forsake and deny.
Thy game liketh me not at all.

EVERYMAN:

Why then, ye will forsake me all?
Sweet *Strength,* tarry a little space.

STRENGTH:

Nay, sir, by the rood of grace!
I will hie me from thee fast,
Though thou weep till thy heart to burst.

EVERYMAN:

Ye would ever bide by me, ye said.

STRENGTH:

Yea, I have you far enough conveyed!
Ye be old enough, I understand,
Your pilgrimage to take on hand.
I repent me that I hither came.

EVERYMAN:

Strength, you to displease I am to blame.
Will ye break promise that is debt?

STRENGTH:
In faith I care not.
Thou art but a fool to complain.
You spend your speech and waste your brain.
Go thrust thee into the ground!

STRENGTH *goes.*

EVERYMAN:
I had weened surer I should you have found.
He that trusteth in his *Strength*
She him deceiveth at the length.
Both *Strength* and *Beauty* forsaketh me;
Yet they promised me fair and lovingly.

DISCRETION:
Everyman, I will after *Strength* be gone.
As for me I will leave you alone.

EVERYMAN:
Why, *Discretion,* will ye forsake me?

DISCRETION:
Yea, in faith, I will go from thee;
For when *Strength* goeth before,
I follow after evermore.

EVERYMAN:
Yet I pray thee for the love of the Trinity,
Look in my grave once piteously.

DISCRETION:
Nay, so nigh, will I not come.
Farewell, everyone!

DISCRETION *goes.*

EVERYMAN:
O, all thing faileth, save God alone—

Beauty, Strength, and *Discretion;*
For when *Death* bloweth his blast
They all run from me full fast.

FIVE WITS:
Everyman, my leave now of thee I take.
I will follow the other, for here I thee forsake.

EVERYMAN:
Alas then may I wail and weep,
For I took you for my best friend.

FIVE WITS:
I will no longer thee keep.
Now farewell, and there an end.

> FIVE WITS *goes.* EVERYMAN *is on his knees at the*
> *entrance to the Grave,* DEATH *standing over him.*

EVERYMAN:
O Jesus help! All hath forsaken me!

GOOD DEEDS:
Nay, *Everyman,* I will bide with thee.
I will not forsake thee indeed.
Thou shalt find me a good friend at need.

EVERYMAN:
Gramercy, *Good Deeds!* Now may I true friends see.
They have forsaken me, everyone.
I loved them better than my *Good Deeds* alone.
Knowledge, will ye forsake me also?

KNOWLEDGE:
Yea, *Everyman,* when ye to death shall go;
But not yet for no manner of danger.

EVERYMAN: Gramercy, *Knowledge,* with all my heart.

KNOWLEDGE:
Nay, yet I will not from hence depart
Till I see where ye shall be come.

EVERYMAN:
Methink, alas, that I must be gone
To make my reckoning, and my debts pay;
For I see my time is nigh spent away.
Take example, all ye that this do hear or see
How they that I loved best do forsake me,
Except my *Good Deeds* that bideth truly.

GOOD DEEDS:
All earthly things is but vanity.
Beauty, Strength, and *Discretion* do man forsake,
Foolish friends and kinsmen that fair spake
All fleeth save *Good Deeds,* and that am I.

EVERYMAN:
Have mercy on me, God most mighty,
And stand by me thou mother and maid, Holy Mary.

GOOD DEEDS:
Fear not. I will speak for thee.

EVERYMAN:
Hear I cry God mercy.

GOOD DEEDS:
Shorten our end and 'minish our pain!
Let us go, and never come again.

EVERYMAN:
Into thy hands, Lord, my soul I commend.
Receive it, Lord, that it be not lost.
As thou me boughtest, so me defend,
And save me from the fiend's boast,
That I may appear with that blessed host

That shall be saved at the day of doom.
In manus tuas of mightës most.
For ever *commendo spiritum meum.*

> EVERYMAN *and* GOOD DEEDS *follow* DEATH *into the Grave.*

KNOWLEDGE:
Now hath he suffered that we all shall endure.
The *Good Deeds* shall make all sure.
Now hath he made ending.

> *The choir sings an Allelujah chorus.*

Methinketh that I hear angels sing
And make great joy and melody
Where *Everyman's* soul received shall be.

> KNOWLEDGE *goes out. An* ANGEL *enters, to the stage of God.*

ANGEL:
Come, excellent elect spouse to Jesu!
Here above thou shalt go
Because of thy singular virtue.
Now the soul is taken the body from,
Thy reckoning is crystal clear.
Now shalt thou into the heavenly sphere
Unto the which all ye shall come
That liveth well before the day of doom.

> *The singing ends.* KNOWLEDGE *goes. The* DOCTOR *enters.*

DOCTOR:
This moral men may have in mind.
Ye hearers, take it of worth, old and young,
And forsake pride, for he deceiveth you in the end;
And remember *Beauty, Five Wits, Strength,* and *Discretion,*
They all at last do *Everyman* forsake,
Save his *Good Deeds* there doth he take.

But beware and they be small,
Before God he hath no help at all.
None excuse may there be for *Everyman.*
Alas, how shall he do then?
For after death amends may no man make,
For then mercy and pity doth him forsake.
If his reckoning be not clear when he doth come,
God will say, *Ite maledicti in ignem æternum!*
And he that hath his account whole and sound,
High in Heaven he shall be crowned.
Unto which place God bring us all thither
That we may live body and soul together.
Thereto help, the Trinity!
Amen, say ye, for Saint Charity.

FINIS

Thus endeth the moral play of Everyman.

Medieval Plays in Modern Production
by E. MARTIN BROWNE

General

The medieval plays have been revived with success many times in recent years, both in Britain and in America. Interest in them has grown so considerably over the past thirty or forty years that it was possible at the Festival of Britain in 1951 to stage a compressed version of the whole of the York cycle as the main event of the York festival. This production met with such great success that it was repeated in 1954 and again, in a slightly altered form, in 1957. Correspondingly in Chester, productions of the Chester cycle were staged in 1951 and 1957, and in Coventry the two remaining plays of the genuine Coventry cycle were staged in 1951. With large numbers of productions in churches, in the open air, in halls by smaller groups, the plays are now becoming once more a part of the currency of English dramatic literature. There is no reason, then, why these plays should not be valid for modern audiences. That they are strange in certain respects, in language and in their approach to their subject, does not invalidate the strength of their faith nor their artistic power.

Those who produce them, must, however, think in terms of the original creation and not in terms of a modernization to suit their own ideas. Above all I would urge producers not to think of the plays as quaint. They are simple, direct and strong. The director should not exploit the differences in manners between the Middle Ages and today, but should build upon the common belief which underlies both civilizations, and give the plays the opportunity to put forward their message in as powerful a way as they did originally. The sturdy faith which the plays contain is their best recommendation to an audience—whether composed of believers or not. It is a faith for weekdays, and should not wear the pious air of a faith for Sundays only. The people lived by it, they took it for granted as the basis of their lives. Accordingly the performances should be strong and, although full of devotion, not of a sickly or sentimental kind.

These plays have been compared, not without reason, to the work of the contemporary playwright Berthold Brecht. They share with his plays the deliberate avoidance of emotion for emotion's sake, the deliberate attempt to present their matter as factual truth. For the truths of the Christian faith are facts to the medieval author and actor just as the truths of Communism are facts to Berthold Brecht.

Style and Behavior

The action of the Mystery Play is imagined as happening directly to the people taking part in it; any idea of what we call period is entirely absent. Although it is hard for us, perhaps, to divorce ourselves from our modern conceptions and put ourselves back into the medieval mind, we must attempt to do so. This involves the complete omission from the production of everything to do with oriental Palestine or with Rome or Judaism. It involves seeing everything in terms of medieval English life, and finding for those characters which in modern biblical 'period' plays would be clothed in Palestinian or in Roman or Jewish garb, their counterparts in the life of medieval society. The instances of the high priests being transformed into bishops and Pilate into a great lord have already been given: and everything in the plays should be considered in these terms. (It is much easier to grasp this if a study is made of contemporary medieval art, where the same process has been at work.) Furthermore, one must understand that this method of looking at the story is quite unselfconscious. As it was completely natural to the medieval author and his actors so it does not demand of modern actors any selfconscious medievalism in performance, but rather an attempt to behave naturally in terms of the life of the time.

This life was lived in an integrated society. One of our difficulties as modern actors is that our society is not at all integrated. The gangling walk in which the limbs seem to be detached from the body, so typical of many of the younger actors today, expresses a relationship to society which is completely absent from medieval life. The medieval man, however humble his station, grew up thinking of his body as a single whole, thinking of himself as belonging to a single society serving those who were over him and doing the work that he was called upon to do. Accordingly his behavior has no pretense about it and, equally, no sloppiness. Elaborate courtliness should be completely absent from the medieval Mystery Plays, except where it is being used for purposes of satire: for instance, in the scene of the trial of Jesus before Herod, the king and his family are represented as speaking French, the courtly language, in order to differentiate them from the more robust "English" court of Pilate. This is popular drama, we cannot insist too strongly, and we must try to put ourselves in the position of the ordinary medieval man for whom the plays had been written and through whose eyes everything in them was seen.

The problem of costume will be approached with this in mind. The costumes will of course be of the period of the plays' writing, that is to say between 1350 and 1450. The clothes of the minor characters will be very simple, rough, sometimes skimpy, based upon the jerkin, the hood and the stockings (or, as we call them, 'tights'). They will mostly be of the color of earth; and in fact, a great variety of shade can be introduced into such a scheme. It is a mistake to color the whole stage too brightly in a medieval production. The minor characters should form the background for the major characters, who should shine forth from the center of the scene like brilliantly colored jewels. The background will consist of the colors of the earth worn by men of the earth, and the color of steel worn by the soldiers in chain armour, which, by the way, should not be polished. The bright colors of the principal characters will be augmented by the much greater amount of material in their clothing. This is a feudal society, in which strict degrees of order are adhered to, and those who stand in high place not only can afford, but also are obliged to dress in rich and ample materials. Such scenes as those of the three kings and of Pilate's family should be brilliant to look upon; other scenes, such as those of the shepherds or of Peter's denial or of Gethsemane, should be altogether more subdued in tone. Jesus Himself is always clothed in white. Adam and Eve traditionally wore white leather. This is not easy to achieve successfully in modern production, but a convention must be found for them, and for Jesus during the Crucifixion scenes, which will satisfy both decorum and artistic taste. God the Father is always represented as a great king with a triple or high-pointed crown and a great canopy highly decorated with gold and jewels. The angels in medieval paintings usually had wings, but their garments were in fact derived from the ecclesiastical alb and dalmatic of the church service, and they can quite well be clothed in these without wings if desired. Wings in a production where there is movement present grave problems. As a basis for the study of this question of costume, the book *Dressing the Play* by Miss Norah Lambourne, who designed the York Mystery Cycle production, will be found particularly helpful.

Staging

For modern production the plays can be staged in a variety of ways:

a) *Reviving the Pageant*—The pageant cart which has been described earlier in the book can be revived, but only of course in special circumstances. At York in 1954, the play of Noah's Flood was given on a pageant at two stations in the city, and, in 1957, the play of the Red Sea. For these a railway wagon was used measuring sixteen feet by six. On it was built in the first case an ark, sixteen feet by three, and in the second case a throne for Pharaoh, the other scenes being suggested by removable properties. This experiment was entirely successful as a means of restoring to our knowledge the quality of the original popular show, but it does not give scope for a large audience to enjoy the Mystery Plays as a whole nor for the actors to display their full talents. To do justice to these texts it is necessary to have an auditorium with seats and with enough space to deploy the series of plays one after the other.

b) *Mansions on the Open Stage*—At York, therefore, the main production was given in the following manner. The ruins of the Abbey Church of St. Mary were used, with five arches of the north wall and the northwest corner as background to the stage. Across the corner was built a large triangular platform stage, six feet six inches from the ground, allowing beneath it the sepulchre of Christ and staging on it such scenes as the creation and fall of man, Gethsemane, the Crucifixion, etc. From the stage was built into the corner a stairway which led up from Earth to Heaven. Heaven was in the series of clere-storey windows twenty feet from the ground, and in the central one of the five was the throne of God the Father. On either side of Him the windows were used for the angels and for Christ at the Last Judgement. Access from Earth to Heaven was provided by the corner staircase. On the green sward below at the far end of the stage stood the mouth of Hell, so that the conflict between good and evil, presided over by Almighty God in the center, stretched from the Way to Heaven on one side to the Mouth of Hell on the other.

In 1951 and 1954 there were inserted, between these two, the 'mansions' which were the houses of Pilate, of the Nativity and of the high priests. In 1957, there was substituted for these a central neutral stage called, in the words of the play, "middle Earth," which could be adapted by the use of properties and banners to represent a variety of places. This type of staging allowed for very swift movement and complete continuity, so that it was possible to stage the whole of the history of Man in this compressed form in three hours and a half without any break save one for convenience after the Palm Sunday play. Some such staging as this is necessary in modern productions if the sweep of the story is to be maintained and the audience's interest is to be held throughout.

A similar production of the Chester plays was given at Bryanston School in 1955. At Chester the plays are staged in the ancient refectory of the monastery, a smallish building, which necessitates the production being rather more static; but even so, as swift a movement as possible is maintained between the various scenes. This of course involves dovetailing the various one-act plays of the cycle into each other, by cutting off, so to speak, their heads and tails.

c) *Church*—The Mystery Plays are admirably adapted for production in church, and have been used in this way very widely in recent times. The very fact that they were not written for a scenic stage makes them all the more suitable. To give the best idea of the kind of treatment which they may receive, let me describe a production of the Nativity section of the York cycle in the Chapel of Union Theological Seminary at Christmas, 1956.

This Chapel has a raised chancel with an open space between the choir stalls, at the head of which stands the Communion table. On the left is the pulpit, which with its approach is almost ten feet wide, wide enough therefore to house a separate scene, and on the right is the lectern where there is seven feet of playing space. Thus it is possible to divide the chancel area into different scenes, and diversify the interest as well as clarify the play by attaching certain characters to certain parts of the playing space. The pulpit was used for the house of Mary and Joseph at Nazareth, and for the house of Herod; the lectern for the house of Elizabeth and the house of Simeon; the Communion table was used for the altar in the Temple at the presentation of the child Jesus, and the central area in front of it was used for the Nativity and for those scenes which, starting from a particular location, overflowed into the central space. This is in accordance with medieval practice, as has been seen. The method used at York is the method used in all southern English and Continental productions of the Mystery Plays in the Middle Ages. In a church it has the further advantage that the play becomes a procession, that characters move up and down the aisles from place to place, and although they return to almost the same area, the area at which the audience is looking, their movement has registered the change of place.

In some churches it is possible to use more than one stage, and very interesting and beautiful effects can be gained by placing small stages at two or three different locations in the church. This again leads to processional production. No screening is used for the stage, and any shifting of properties is done in view of the audience by suitably trained actors. No background is provided other than the natural background of the church building itself, where the story is completely at home, since it is the story of the religion for which the church was built.

d) *Hall*—If the plays are produced in a hall or theatre, the use of tableau curtains, front curtains and fully set scenery should be avoided as much as possible. An attempt should be made to simplify in the direction of the staging of the original production, making use of properties and effects, both of which were very dear to the medieval heart, rather than of scenery, which was unknown in the Middle Ages. Before a neutral background a satisfactory flow of action can, with a little imaginative ingenuity, be maintained.

Acting

All the parts in the plays were originally taken by men and boys. This today would only be desirable in a boys' school or college, for it is necessary to give both sexes an opportunity in a production of this kind. This is not as difficult as it may seem, for apart from the specifically female parts, some of the others, minor characters such as porters, citizens, etc., can be converted without very much difficulty. It should, however, be urged upon all, whether male or female, that their acting must have the strength and directness which belong to the plays. It will help them if, in the early stages of rehearsal, they become accustomed to the kind of movement which is characteristic of medieval people, particularly the women and the characters of higher station among the men. These are going to have to carry costumes with a considerable amount of material in them, and they should learn to enjoy doing so and to use their costumes as a means of making themselves walk in the proper manner. A free, regular walk with the shoulders held straight and the head well poised is essential to acting these parts. This can be practised before rehearsal, but it will help actors additionally if they can have the use of their costumes at an early stage, in order that the costume itself may teach them something about what their deportment should be.

The delivery of the lines will perhaps present problems to actors unaccustomed to playing in verse, especially as the language will often be somewhat unfamiliar. It is a good rule to look for the key word in each sentence and make sure that that word, whatever else, reaches the audience with force; the sentence will then shape itself around the key word and carry the line along. Actors should not be afraid of rhyme; they should not stress it for its own sake, but they will often find it helpful in conveying their point. The author has not meant the point to be obscured, nor to convey the impression (too often given in productions of Shakespeare, as well of earlier dramatists) that the play really ought to have been written in prose. The pattern of the verse is one of the joys of the play and should be enjoyed by the actor, who should convey that enjoyment to the audience.

Despite its sorrows and difficulties, the medieval period was gay, and performances of these plays which do not reflect this gaiety do them scant justice, as well as making them much less entertaining to an audience. The whole proceeding should be infused with a light and airy grace and the actors should feel themselves to be taking part in a festival, as indeed, in the original production, they were every year.

Music

Music should be contemporary with the plays so far as this can be achieved. There is still not a large body of fourteenth- and fifteenth-century music available for ordinary use, nor very many people who know how to sing it. If any expert can be persuaded to assist with the production, this will be invaluable in giving the plays the right atmosphere. They are meant to have the assistance of a considerable amount of music, some of which is indicated in the script.

The two sources from which music can most easily be drawn are these:

1) The carols of the period. The best collection is the *Oxford Carol Book,* and from this it is necessary to pick out those which are genuinely old and preferably those which are English, though some of those from Continental countries may well come into use. One or two of the modern composers, notably Ralph Vaughan-Williams, Gustav Holst and Martin Shaw, have caught the spirit of medieval carols particularly well, and their original work can be used without too much incongruity. It is absolutely necessary to avoid the use of work from the seventeenth, eighteenth and nineteenth centuries, and even though the director may have particular favorites among carols of these periods, he should deny himself the pleasure of using them with a medieval play.

2) The other source is plainsong, the liturgical music of the Church. This is indicated for use at a number of points in the plays and will be suitable in a good many more. *Vexilla Regis,* for instance, on the way to the cross, *Dies Irae* at the Last Judgement, etc. Here again it is necessary to find an expert who understands the performance of plainsong and can provide the right muisc from his knowledge. Most Roman Catholic churches can suggest such a one, though he must be urged to use the

original sources rather than the modernized versions which are all too common in church services today.

If these two sources are well used they should provide all that is necessary, but it is most desirable that directors of these plays should keep their eyes and ears open for the emergence of further music of the period, of which there is a very great store, only now being edited.

The music should be performed with a lightness, a spring in the rhythm, and a gaiety, in the carols particularly, which will match the performance of the play. It is worth remembering that the carols are of the same *genre* as folk dance, and that their performance should have something of the movement of the dance about it.

SCRIPTS AND BIBLIOGRAPHY

The primary question has been left to the last, because the best answer to it is given in the light of the approach to production suggested in the foregoing. What version is to be used? The best method, and not such a difficult one as it may seem, is for the director to make his own selection of material from good editions of the medieval texts, to suit the conditions of his production. He can thus be sure that his text fits the stage and the type of cast he is using, and gives a program of the desired length; and he can plan the physical shape of the production, the addition of music, etc., to suit his circumstances.

In handling the scripts, he should try to make himself as familiar with, and as sensitive as possible to, the qualities of the original: for he can quickly destroy these qualities if he cuts and twists the text in too arbitrary a manner. His aim must be to give his modern audience the opportunity to experience the impact of the medieval plays, rather than to create for his audience what he thinks they want or will be able to take. His editing, in selection as well as in language, will thus be directed toward providing the bridge over which, so to speak, they can walk into the Middle Ages and partake of the life they find there. In doing this, the modern director will among other things be speeding up the tempo at which the plays unfold their material; but he will be doing this, if he is wise, rather by joining together the separate pieces of the medieval script than by hacking parts of it away altogether. Much of the didactic speechifying will be removed; for we are accustomed to a faster flow of action than was the original audience, and are more likely to accept what the plays have to say by implication than as direct statement.

By way of bibliography, I will begin by listing the most useful editions to work from.

THE YORK CYCLE OF MYSTERY PLAYS (S.P.C.K., London; Macmillan, New York) by Dr. J. S. Purvis, is a complete version of the forty-eight plays, made by the York scholar who prepared the stage scripts for the revivals at the York Festival. This is the authoritative text for this cycle.

THE YORK NATIVITY PLAY (S.P.C.K.) by E. Martin Browne, is an earlier and more freely adapted version of the Nativity scenes. This should be used only as a guide to a director, who should adapt his text from Dr. Purvis' better and fuller version. The usefulness of this little book is in the suggestions it gives of how to prepare a production for a church.

THE PLAY OF THE MAID MARY and THE PLAY OF MARY THE MOTHER (S.P.C.K.) are similar adaptations of the Hegge cycle by E. Martin Browne, and may have a similar usefulness.

THE CHESTER MYSTERY PLAYS (Heinemann) by Maurice Hussey, is a careful adaptation of the Chester cycle, reducing it to a size which would bring it within the scope of a modern production. This is the best text available for this cycle.

THE NORWICH PASSION PLAY (Wherry Press, 14 Heigham Street, Norwich, England), from the Hegge cycle, was prepared for the Maddermarket Theatre, Norwich, 1939.

To these should be added the best small collection of original texts (the spelling is modernized), to which I have been much indebted and which affords the best introduction to a scholarly treatment of the material:

EVERYMAN AND MEDIAEVAL MIRACLE PLAYS (Dent, Everyman edition), edited by Dr. A. C. Cawley.

The standard authority for a study of the whole subject is ENGLISH RELIGIOUS DRAMA IN THE MIDDLE AGES by Dr. Hardin Craig (Oxford). This admirably balanced and profoundly understanding work incorporates the essentials of the earlier work of Sir Edmund Chambers in his great book THE MEDIAEVAL STAGE, and of other scholars.

The Middle English texts from which the editions listed above have been made will only be of use to those who have some acquaintance with the old form of the language. They are as follows:

Early English Text Society:
No. 120, Extra Series, *Ludus Coventriae* (Hegge cycle), ed. K. S. Block.
No. 87, Extra Series, *Two Coventry Corpus Christi Plays* (the real Coventry plays), ed. Hardin Craig.
Nos. 62 and 115, Extra Series, *The Chester Plays*, ed. Deimling and Matthews.
Nos. 71, Extra Series, *The Towneley Plays* (Wakefield cycle), ed. England and Pollard.
No. 104, Extra Series, *The Non-Cycle Mystery Plays,* ed. O. Waterhouse.
Oxford University Press:
York Mystery Plays, ed. L. Toulmin Smith.

LIVING AGE BOOKS

published by MERIDIAN BOOKS, INC.
12 East 22 Street, New York 10, New York